JOSEPH F MICELI JR

Launch Your A.I. Based Business Today

Launch Smart, Scale Fast, Succeed!

CYBICUS
PUBLISHING

First edition

ISBN: 979-8-9919701-6-7

Editing by Nytalya Frye

Contents

Launch Your A.I.-Based Business Today: Launch Smart, Scale Fast, Succeed!

By: Joseph F Miceli Jr

* * *

Introduction

Artificial intelligence is reshaping how we work, create, and solve problems. What was once exclusively the realm of large corporations or research institutions is now available to entrepreneurs, freelancers, and small businesses. Thanks to no-code and low-code platforms, AI-driven products and services can be built, tested, and launched faster and more affordably than ever. With this, the barriers have fallen and now, any motivated person can turn an AI-based problem-solving ideas into a thriving business. The future is changing and you can be a part of it. *Peter Drucker said,* "The best way to predict the future is to create it." With this book as your guide I predict you will have the tools to create the future.

This book, is a practical road map for doers, dreamers, and innovators who want to define real-world problems, leverage powerful AI technologies, and build companies that deliver meaningful solutions. Whether you, are a technical newbie or an experienced founder, this book will guide you step by step; from clarifying your niche, through selecting the right tools and validating your idea, to launching, scaling, and systematizing your business.

We'll begin by focusing on essentials: how to pinpoint urgent problems worth solving and which AI tools and agent technologies are most relevant to non-technical founders. You will also learn how to identify your target customers, determine the best business models, and create simple prototypes to test your ideas quickly before investing significant time or money.

As you progress, you will discover how to brand your venture, take care of legal and structural aspects, and set up the workflows that power modern AI-driven businesses, all while maintaining agility and ease of iteration. Specific case studies and actionable frameworks will demystify every phase, from first experiments to market launch and early growth.

This book is especially mindful of the operational realities of building in the AI space: automating repetitive tasks, organizing feedback loops, utilizing market data, and adapting as technology and customer needs evolve. You'll find checklists for legal setup, tool selection, user feedback, and KPIs, along with guidance for hiring and managing your first team members, if and when you scale.

Most importantly, *Launch Your A.I. Based Business Today: Launch Smart, Scale Fast, Succeed!*, champions a hands-on, iterative approach. Start small, test thoughtfully, and measure your wins. The world doesn't need another theoretical take on AI in business. It needs builders, people who use today's accessible technology to create tomorrow's solutions. If you're ready to start, let us dive in.

* * *

1

Discover Your Niche

Every great business begins not with a solution, but with a problem. Before a single line of code is written, a product is designed, or an AI agent is configured, a successful entrepreneur identifies a genuine, nagging issue that people are actively trying to solve. In the world of AI-based businesses, this principle is even more critical. The power of artificial intelligence is vast, but without a specific, well-defined target, that power is wasted. It can be equated to the difference between a laser beam and a floodlight. A floodlight illuminates a wide area, but a laser can cut through steel. Your goal in this chapter is to find the point where you will focus your energy to create a business with surgical precision.

This focused problem area is your niche. A niche isn't just a demographic, like small business owners, or a market, like fitness. It's a specific problem experienced by a specific group of people. Helping freelance graphic designers automate the creation of social media content variants for their clients is a niche, AI for marketing is not. The former is a tangible problem with a clear audience; the latter is a vague idea. A strong niche gives you a clear direction for what to build, who to sell to, and how to communicate your value. It's the foundational step upon which your entire business will be built.

Many aspiring founders fall into the "solution-first" trap. They get excited about a new technology, perhaps a new AI model or a no-code platform, and immediately start brainstorming all the "cool things" it could do. This approach is backward and often leads to building products nobody wants. The alternative is the problem-first mindset. Instead of asking, "What can I build with AI?" you should be asking, "What frustrating, time-consuming, or expensive problem can be made better with AI?" This shift in perspective is the most important mental adjustment you will make on your entrepreneurial journey.

Passion is a key ingredient in this process. You're going to be dedicating a significant portion of your life to solving this problem, so you should have a genuine interest in the domain. However, passion alone is not a business plan. Your passion for vintage science-fiction novels is wonderful, but it doesn't automatically translate into a viable business. The magic happens when your passion overlaps with a problem that other people have and, crucially, are willing to pay to solve. Your enthusiasm will fuel you through the hard times, but the market's need for a solution is what will fuel your revenue.

The Anatomy of a Powerful Niche

To separate a fleeting idea from a genuine business opportunity, you need to dissect the problem you are considering. The best niches have a few things in common: they address a problem that is not just annoying, but urgent; they offer a solution that provides clear, measurable value; and they target a group of people who are already demonstrating a willingness to spend money to alleviate their pain. Now, let us break down these components.

First, consider the urgency of the problem. Is it a "hair-on-fire" problem or a "nice-to-have" solution? A "hair-on-fire" problem is something that causes immediate and significant pain. It might be a process that is losing a company thousands of dollars each week, a regulatory requirement that carries heavy fines if ignored, or a customer support bottleneck that is leading to public complaints and churn. People with "hair-on-fire" problems are actively, desperately searching for a solution right now. They don't need to be convinced they have a problem; they are acutely aware of it.

A "nice-to-have" solution, on the other hand, addresses a minor inconvenience. An AI that suggests a new, exotic coffee bean to try each morning might be interesting, but it doesn't solve a burning problem. When budgets get tight, "nice-to-haves" are the first things to be cut. "Hair-on-fire" problems, however, demand a solution regardless of the economic climate. For example, a business facing a data breach needs a cybersecurity solution urgently, making it a high-priority issue. Your goal is to find a problem that keeps your target customer awake at night.

Next, you must have a clear value proposition. What is the tangible, undeniable benefit that your AI-based solution will provide? A strong value proposition can usually be expressed in terms of saving money, making money, or saving significant amounts of time. Vague promises like "improving efficiency" or "streamlining workflows" are not enough. You need to be specific. Will your solution reduce the time it takes to do a specific task by 50%? Will it increase sales leads by 15%? Will it cut operational costs by a measurable dollar amount?

The clearer your value proposition, the easier it will be to sell your product. A customer should be able to look at your offering and immediately understand how it will improve their business or life. For example, instead of "AI for project management," a stronger value proposition would be "An AI agent that attends your Zoom meetings and automatically generates and assigns action items, saving each project manager 5 hours per week." The value is specific, measurable, and directly tied to a painful, time-consuming task. This is the kind of clarity that makes a customer pull out their credit card.

Finally, you must assess the customer's willingness to pay. It is a harsh truth that people complain about many problems they have no intention of ever paying to solve. A great indicator of willingness to pay is to see if people are already spending money on the problem, even if they are using imperfect, clunky, or inefficient solutions. Are they hiring freelancers, buying complex software and only using 10% of its features, or manually stitching together multiple spreadsheets to achieve a poor version of the outcome you can provide?

If a market is already spending money on a problem, you don't have to validate the existence of a budget for it. You just have to convince them that your solution is better, faster, or cheaper than what they're currently using. This is a far easier task than trying to create a new market from scratch and educating people on why they should start paying for something they have always done for free or simply ignored.

Techniques for Discovering Your Niche

Now that you know what a good niche looks like, how do you find one? The good news is that potential business ideas are all around you. You just need to learn how to see them. This involves shifting your mindset from a passive consumer to an active problem-hunter. The following techniques will help you systematically uncover and evaluate niche opportunities.

Start With Your Own Problems

The most authentic and often most successful business ideas come from personal experience. This approach is often called "scratching your own itch." What are the daily frustrations and inefficiencies you face in your own job or personal life? What tasks are so repetitive and tedious that you wish a robot would just do them for you? What information do you constantly find yourself struggling to find, organize, or make sense of? These personal pain points are fantastic starting points because you are already an expert in the problem.

Think about your industry. Are there outdated processes that have survived simply because "that's how it's always been done"? Do you use software that makes you want to throw your computer out the window? Do you spend hours on manual data entry, cross-referencing documents, or preparing reports? Each of these frustrations is a potential AI business in disguise. An AI tool could potentially automate that data entry, instantly cross-reference those documents, or generate that report in seconds.

Keep a "problem journal" for a week. Every time you feel a moment of frustration with a task, write it down. Be specific. Don't just write "paperwork is annoying." Write "It takes me 45 minutes to find the relevant clauses in three different contracts and copy them into a new client proposal." At the end of the week, review your list. Do you see any patterns? Are any of these problems experienced by others in your field? If so, you may have just found the seed of your new business.

Become a Digital Eavesdropper

Your future customers are already talking about their problems online. Your job is to find them and listen. Online forums, social media groups, and Q&A sites are goldmines of unfiltered customer pain points. People go to these places to vent their frustrations and ask for help, providing you with a direct window into their needs.

Platforms like Reddit are particularly valuable. Find the "subreddits" (niche forums) where your potential customers congregate. If you're interested in helping real estate agents, spend time in 'r/RealEstate'. If you're targeting small e-commerce store owners, browse 'r/ecommerce'. Look for posts and comments containing phrases like "How do I deal with...", "I'm so tired of...", "Does anyone have a tool that...", or "What's the best way to..." These are cries for help and clear indicators of unsolved problems.

Quora is another excellent resource. It is a platform built entirely around questions and answers. Search for topics related to your areas of interest and look at the questions people are asking. The most popular questions with hundreds of answers often point to widespread and persistent problems. LinkedIn Groups can provide more professional and B2B (Business to Business) focused discussions, while specialized industry forums can offer deep, domain-specific insights.

When you find these conversations, don't just read them. Analyze them. What specific language do people use to describe their problems? What solutions have they already tried? What are their frustrations with those existing solutions? Create a simple spreadsheet to track the problems you find, the forums where you found them, and any interesting quotes or details. This qualitative data is invaluable for understanding the market's true needs.

Use Keyword Research as a Problem Radar

Every day, millions of people type their problems into Google. With basic keyword research, you can analyze what they're searching for, giving you a quantitative measure of demand for a potential solution. Keyword research isn't just for SEO experts; it's a powerful market research tool that can help you validate your niche.

Start by brainstorming the phrases people might use to search for a solution to a problem you've identified. Think beyond product names and focus on the problem itself. For example, instead of "CRM software," a potential customer might search for "how to track sales leads" or "best way to manage customer contacts." These problem-based keywords are what you want to investigate.

You can use free tools like the Google Keyword Planner (you'll need a Google account) or simply pay attention to Google's own autosuggest feature to get ideas. As you type a search query, Google will show you a list of related searches, which can reveal how other people are thinking about the problem.

For more detailed analysis, tools like Ahrefs, SEMrush, or GrowthBar can provide data on monthly search volume for specific keywords.

High search volume for a problem-based keyword is a strong signal that many people are experiencing that pain point. It's a direct measure of demand. For example, if you find that "how to automate client on-boarding" has thousands of searches per month, you know you've tapped into a significant and widespread need. Conversely, if nobody is searching for the problem you're trying to solve, it might be a sign that it's not as painful or prevalent as you thought.

The Power of Talking to Humans

While online research is powerful, nothing replaces a direct conversation. Conducting informational interviews with people in your target market is the single most effective way to understand their problems, motivations, and willingness to pay. The key to a successful customer discovery interview is to listen, not to pitch. Your goal is to learn about their world, not to sell them on your brilliant idea.

Identify five to ten people who fit your potential customer profile. You can find them through your personal network, LinkedIn, or even by reaching out to people in the online forums you've been monitoring. Ask them for 20 minutes of their time to discuss their experiences in their industry. Emphasize that you are not selling anything; you are simply doing research.

During the interview, ask open-ended questions that encourage them to tell stories. Instead of asking, "Is invoicing a problem for you?", which can be answered with a simple "yes" or "no," ask, "Can you tell me about the last time you had to send out invoices? What was that process like?" Listen for emotion. When does their voice change? When do you hear frustration, anger, or exhaustion? These emotional cues often point to the most significant pain points.

Here are some powerful questions to guide your conversations:

"What's the most frustrating part of your workday?"

"What tasks take up a disproportionate amount of your time?"

"What are you currently using to solve [problem X]? What do you like and dislike about

it?"

"If you had a magic wand and could eliminate one task from your to-do list forever, what

would it be?"

"Have you ever tried to find a better solution for [problem X]? What happened?"

Take meticulous notes and, if possible, have a partner join you to observe and take notes so you can focus on the conversation. The insights you gain from these conversations are pure gold. They will not only help you validate or invalidate your niche but will also give you the exact language to use in your marketing and sales materials later on.

The Final Check: Is Your Niche a Winner?

After going through these discovery exercises, you will likely have a list of several promising niche ideas. Now, it's time to evaluate them and choose a front runner to move forward with. A simple scoring matrix can help you objectively compare your options and make a data-informed decision rather than relying on a gut feeling.

Create a simple table and list your niche ideas in the first column. Then, create columns for a few key criteria. For each idea, score it on a scale of 1 to 5 for each of the following:

1. Problem Urgency: How much pain does this problem cause? (1 = Minor annoyance, 5 =

Hair-on-fire, critical issue)

2. Value Proposition Clarity: How easy is it to explain the tangible benefit? (1 = Vague, 5 =

Crystal clear benefit like saving time/money)

3. Willingness to Pay: Are people already spending money in this area? (1 = No one pays

for this, 5 = A large, established budget exists)

4. Market Size: Roughly how many people or businesses have this problem? (1 = Very few,

5 = A very large, addressable market)

5. Personal Passion/Expertise: How interested are you in this area? (1 = Not at all, 5 = I

could talk about this all day)

Let's imagine you're comparing two ideas: "AI-powered recipe generator for home cooks" and "AI-powered tool for small law firms to automate deposition summaries." The recipe generator might score highly on market size and personal passion, but it would likely score low on urgency and willingness to pay. The deposition summary tool, while having a smaller market, would score extremely high on urgency (a lawyers' time is expensive), value proposition (saving hours of high-cost labor), and willingness to pay (law firms are used to paying for efficiency tools). The legal tool is the much stronger business candidate.

This exercise isn't meant to give you a single "correct" answer, but to force you to think critically about the business potential of each idea. The goal is not to find a perfect score across the board, but to identify the idea with the strongest combination of high urgency and a clear, valuable solution for a market that is ready and willing to pay.

Once you have analyzed your options and chosen a primary niche to focus on, you are ready for the next phase. You have a well-defined, urgent problem in hand, and you have strong evidence that a market exists for a solution. The next step is to explore the landscape of AI tools and platforms that can help you build that solution, bringing you one step closer to launching your business.

* * *

2

Mapping the AI Tools & Agent Landscape

Having a well-defined, urgent problem is like having a detailed blueprint for a house. You know what you need to build, who it's for, and why they need it. The next logical question is, what will you build it with? Ten years ago, the answer would have been a team of expensive software developers and months of custom coding. Today, the answer is far more exciting and accessible. As Arthur C. Clarke once said, "Any sufficiently advanced technology is indistinguishable from magic." But as we all know, this is not actual magic, but it is a once in a lifetime opportunity to make technology magic. You're now walking into a vast, well-stocked hardware store filled with powerful, ready-made components. This is the world of no-code and low-code AI platforms, a landscape of incredible tools that let you construct sophisticated solutions without needing a degree in computer science.

This chapter is your guided tour of that hardware store. We will explore the different aisles and tool categories, from intelligent agents that can automate complex workflows to specialized helpers for content, customer service, and data analysis. The goal is not to become an expert on every single tool; the landscape changes too quickly for that. Instead, the goal is to understand the *types* of tools available and to develop a framework for choosing the right ones for your specific problem. You don't need to know how to manufacture a hammer, but you do need to know what a hammer does and when to use it instead of a wrench.

The terms "no-code" and "low-code" are at the heart of this new entrepreneurial era. No-code platforms are exactly what they sound like: tools that allow you to build applications and automate processes using visual interfaces, drag-and-drop editors, and pre-built templates, requiring absolutely no programming. Low-code platforms are a small step up in complexity, perhaps requiring you to write a simple formula or configure a script, but they still handle the vast majority of the technical heavy lifting for you. For the entrepreneur, the distinction is less important than the shared benefit: these platforms manage the complex AI infrastructure, freeing you to focus on solving your customer's problem.

Think of it this way: you don't need to build the power plant (the complex AI models) or wire the city's electrical grid (the cloud infrastructure). You just need to choose the right appliances and plug them into the wall. This chapter will show you where to find the best appliances for the job.

The Major Categories of AI Tools

The world of AI tools can seem chaotic, with new products launching every week. However, most of them can be organized into a few key categories based on their primary function. Understanding these categories is the first step to narrowing your search and finding the right fit for the niche you identified in the previous chapter.

AI Agents and Workflow Automation Platforms

This is arguably the most dynamic and powerful category for building a new AI-based business. An AI agent is more than just a simple automation; it's a system designed to understand a goal, break it down into steps, and use various tools and data sources to accomplish that goal autonomously. Think of it as a tireless, infinitely patient intern you can train to perform complex, multi-step tasks. These platforms are the backbone of businesses that need to automate processes, not just create content.

Platforms in this category provide a visual canvas where you can design these automated workflows. You might drag and drop "nodes" or "blocks" that represent different actions, such as "Read Email," "Extract Invoice Data," "Update CRM," and "Send Confirmation Slack Message." By connecting these blocks, you create a "flow" or "agent" that executes the process automatically.

AI-Powered Workspaces — for Teams, Clients, and Partners

A prime example is FuseBase, which allows you to create AI agents for teams, clients and partners, that live within branded client portals and workspaces. An agent can be trained on your company's knowledge base, documents, and workflows. It can then perform tasks like summarizing meetings, answering client questions based on project files, or even using a browser extension to research information on the web and populate a report. This is ideal for B2B services where you need to provide a secure, collaborative environment for your clients that is supercharged with custom automation.

Other powerful tools in this space include Workato which uses AI to speed up the creation of integrations between over 1,000 different apps, and Gumloop which bills itself as "Zapier with an AI-first approach." These platforms are designed to be the central nervous system of your business operations, connecting different software and orchestrating the flow of data and tasks between them. They are particularly well-suited for solving problems related to internal operations, client onboarding, data processing, and any other process that involves multiple steps and multiple software tools.

Content and Media Generation Assistants

This is the category of AI that has captured the most public attention. These are tools designed to generate original text, images, videos, and even music from simple text prompts. For entrepreneurs, they are incredibly powerful for marketing, content creation, and even as the core component of a product itself. The value proposition is simple: dramatically reduce the time and cost of creating high-quality content.

For text generation, tools like Jasper and Copy.ai have become staples for marketing teams, helping to draft everything from blog posts and social media updates to ad copy and email newsletters. They can be prompted to write in specific tones, for specific audiences, and with specific keywords in mind.

In the realm of visual media, platforms like Midjourney and Stable Diffusion can create stunningly realistic or artistically stylized images from a description. This can be used for blog post illustrations, social media visuals, or product mockups. Similarly, AI video generation APIs can turn a text script into a polished video, complete with a voice-over, which is a massive time-saver for businesses that need to produce video content at scale.

If your business niche involves helping clients with their marketing, communications, or creative processes, these tools will be essential. For example, a business that offers "AI-powered social media management for restaurants" would use text generation tools to create daily posts and image generation tools to create enticing pictures of food specials, all tailored to the restaurant's brand.

Customer Service and Communication Bots

One of the first and most mature applications of commercial AI is in customer support. AI-powered chatbots and communication platforms are designed to handle customer inquiries, answer frequently asked questions, and resolve issues without human intervention by operating 24/7. This frees up human support agents to focus on more complex and high-value interactions.

Platforms like Intercom and Zendesk have deeply integrated AI into their customer communication suites. Their bots can understand the intent behind a customer's question, provide answers from a knowledge base, and, if necessary, intelligently route the conversation to the correct human agent. More specialized tools like Voiceflow or Chatfuel offer no-code visual editors specifically for building these conversational AI agents for websites, messaging apps, or voice assistants.

A business built around these tools might offer "AI-powered customer support setup for e-commerce stores." You would use a platform like Voiceflow to build a custom bot that integrates with the client's Shopify store, answers common questions about order status and return policies, and helps customers find products. This provides a clear value proposition: reduce support ticket volume and increase customer satisfaction.

Data Analysis and Business Intelligence Helpers

Data is the lifeblood of any modern business, but extracting meaningful insights from it has traditionally required specialized skills. No-code business intelligence (BI) tools are changing that by allowing non-technical users to analyze data, create visualizations, and uncover trends. These platforms often let you ask questions about your data in plain English.

Airtable is a standout example of a platform that has blended the simplicity of a spreadsheet with the power of a database and then layered AI on top. With Airtable AI, you can automatically categorize and tag data, summarize customer feedback, or even extract specific information from uploaded documents like invoices or contracts. For instance, a marketing team could use it to analyze survey responses and automatically identify key themes and sentiment trends without manually reading through hundreds of entries.

Other tools in this space, like Metabase and Tableau offer powerful drag-and-drop interfaces for creating interactive dashboards from various data sources. They are designed to make data accessible to everyone in an organization, not just a dedicated data team. A startup built on these tools could offer a service that creates custom, real-time analytics dashboards for a specific industry, such as "inventory and sales forecasting dashboards for independent bookstores." This empowers the client with insights they previously couldn't access.

How to Shortlist the Right Tools for Your Niche

Now that you have a map of the different tool categories, the next task is to select a few potential candidates for your specific business idea. The goal is not to commit to a single platform immediately, but to create a shortlist of two or three promising options that you will test in the next chapter. A systematic approach will save you countless hours and help you avoid choosing a tool that looks great on the surface but doesn't fit your long-term needs.

Step 1: Map Your Core Workflow

Before you even look at a single pricing page, go back to the problem you defined in Chapter 1. On a piece of paper or a whiteboard, map out the step-by-step process of your ideal solution. What is the trigger? What are the inputs? What actions need to happen? What is the final, valuable output?

Let's use the example from Chapter 1: "An AI agent that attends Zoom meetings and automatically generates and assigns action items."

- Trigger: A new meeting recording is available.
- Input: Video/audio file of the meeting, list of attendees.
- Action 1 (AI): Transcribe the entire meeting into text.

- Action 2 (AI): Analyze the transcript to identify action items, responsible persons, and deadlines.
- Action 3 (AI): Format these action items into a structured summary.
- Action 4 (Automation): Send the summary to a shared project management tool (like Asana or Trello) and assign the tasks.
- Output: Action items are created and assigned in the team's project management software.

This simple map is your compass. It tells you exactly what capabilities you need from a tool.

Step 2: Match the Workflow to Tool Categories

Looking at the workflow map, you can now identify which tool categories are most relevant. For our meeting summary example, the core of the solution is a multi-step process involving transcription, analysis, and integration with another tool. This points directly to the AI Agents and Workflow Automation Platforms category. The tool must be able to handle audio files, perform text analysis, and connect to third-party software.

You might also realize you need a tool from a second category. For example, to deliver the service, you might need a simple customer portal where clients can connect their Zoom accounts and manage their settings. This could involve a no-code app builder. For now, focus on the primary engine of your solution.

Step 3: Evaluate Specific Tools with a Decision Matrix

Once you have identified a few potential tools within the right category (e.g., FuseBase, Workato, Make.com), it's time for a head-to-head comparison. Create a simple spreadsheet to score each contender against a set of critical criteria.

Core Feature Fit: How well does the tool's feature set match your workflow map? Can it handle the specific inputs and outputs you need? For our example, does the tool have native video transcription, or would you need to chain together multiple services?

Trial Period & Free Tier: Can you test the core functionality without a significant financial commitment? A generous free trial or a "freemium" plan is essential for rapid experimentation. You need to get your hands on the tool and see if it actually works for your use case.

Pricing & Scalability: Look beyond the introductory price. How does the cost scale? Is it based on the number of users, the number of automated runs ("tasks"), or a flat monthly fee? Ensure the pricing model aligns with how your business will grow. A usage-based model might be cheap to start but could become prohibitively expensive as you gain customers.

Integrations & API: No tool is an island. How easily can it connect to the other applications your customers use? Check for native integrations with popular software (like Google Workspace, Slack, Salesforce). If a native integration doesn't exist, does the platform work with middleware like Zapier, or does it have a well-documented API (Application Programming Interface) that would allow for custom connections down the road?

Ease of Use & Support: How steep is the learning curve for a non-technical founder? Is the interface intuitive? Look for quality documentation, video tutorials, and an active user community or forum. Good support can be a lifesaver when you hit an inevitable roadblock.

Data Security & Privacy: This is non-negotiable, especially if you are handling sensitive client information (as in the legal or medical fields). Review the platform's security policies. Where is data stored? Are they compliant with regulations like GDPR? Do they have features like two-factor authentication and detailed permission controls?

By scoring each potential tool on these criteria, you'll move from a vague sense of "this looks cool" to a data-driven decision about which platforms are the strongest candidates. With this shortlist of well-vetted tools, you are no longer just an observer of the AI revolution. You are now equipped with the knowledge and the components to start building your own solution. The next step is to roll up your sleeves, fire up those free trials, and put your assumptions to the test.

* * *

3

Rapid Experimentation for Fast Validation

You have a problem. You have a handful of tools that claim they can solve it. At this point, many aspiring founders fall into one of two traps. The first is "analysis paralysis," where they spend weeks comparing pricing pages, reading reviews, and creating elaborate feature matrices, never actually trying anything. The second is "premature commitment," where they pick one tool based on its slick marketing, pay for an annual subscription, and spend months trying to force it to work, only to discover a fatal flaw in its logic or a crippling gap in its capabilities. We are going to do neither. We are going to embrace the mindset of a scientist in a lab coat, swapping theory for empirical evidence. *Mark Zuckerberg talking about moving fast once said,* "Move fast and break things. Unless you are breaking stuff, you are not moving fast enough." Welcome to the world of rapid experimentation.

This chapter is about getting your hands dirty. It's about taking your core assumptions about the problem, the solution, and the tools you've shortlisted, and putting them to the test in the fastest, cheapest way possible. The goal here is not to build a finished product or a perfect system. The goal is to get answers. Does the AI actually perform the task you need it to? Is the output valuable? Does the automation save a meaningful amount of time or effort? Answering these questions now, with small, controlled tests, will save you a fortune in wasted time and money down the road. This is the essence of building a lean startup in the age of AI.

Think of each experiment as a focused mission to kill a bad idea before it consumes your resources. If an idea survives this gauntlet of tests, it's because it has merit. A failed experiment isn't a personal failure; it's a success in risk mitigation. It's a data point that tells you to pivot, to try a different tool, or to reconsider your approach. The traditional model of business involved writing a fifty-page business plan and then executing it blindly for a year. The modern, AI-driven approach is to have a series of focused questions and to run a dozen small experiments in a week to answer them. This agility is your single greatest advantage.

The Core of a Lean Experiment: Goal, Input, Output

Every effective experiment, whether in a chemistry lab or a startup, has three fundamental components: a clear goal, a defined input, and a measurable output. Imposing this structure on your tests prevents them from becoming vague, time-consuming "tinkering" sessions and transforms them into focused quests for knowledge. Before you even log into a free trial, you should be able to articulate these three elements for the test you're about to run.

First, you must define a specific Goal. What is the single most important question you are trying to answer with this experiment? A bad goal is broad and fuzzy, like "See what FuseBase can do." A good goal is a sharp, falsifiable hypothesis. It's a question that can be answered with data, not just a feeling. For instance, if your business idea is to automate the creation of real estate property descriptions, a strong experimental goal would be: "Can Tool A generate a 150-word property description from a list of bullet points that is at least 90% factually accurate and requires less than two minutes of human editing?" This goal is specific, measurable, and directly tests the core function of your proposed service.

Next, you must prepare your Input. This is the raw material you will feed into the AI tool to conduct the test. The input should be representative of a real-world scenario, but simple enough to manage for a small-scale experiment. For our real estate example, the input wouldn't be "the entire internet." It would be a curated set of data for a single property: a bulleted list containing the address, square footage, number of bedrooms and bathrooms, key features like "newly renovated kitchen" and "fenced backyard," and perhaps the asking price. Creating a standardized input allows you to run the same test across multiple tools, giving you a true apples-to-apples comparison. Prepare three to five different sets of inputs to ensure your results aren't just a fluke based on one lucky test.

Finally, you must know what Output you expect and how you will measure its success. The output is the tangible result produced by the AI tool after it processes your input. For the property description generator, the output is a block of text. But just getting text back isn't enough; you need metrics to judge its quality. This is where you define your success criteria. You might decide to measure: 1) Factual Accuracy: Did the AI correctly state the number of bedrooms? 2) Completeness: Did it include all the key features from your input list? 3) Readability: Is the text grammatically correct and persuasive? 4) Time-to-Edit: How long does it take a human to polish the output into a client-ready state? By defining these metrics beforehand, you turn a subjective evaluation ("I guess it's okay") into an objective assessment.

The "Wizard of Oz" Technique: Faking It Before You Make It

One of the most powerful forms of rapid experimentation doesn't require you to build a fully automated system at all. It's a technique known as "Wizard of Oz" prototyping. The name comes from the classic movie where the great and powerful Oz was, in reality, just a man behind a curtain pulling levers. In the context of a startup, this means creating the experience of a fully functional, automated AI service for a customer, while you are manually doing the work in the background using the tools you are testing. It's the ultimate way to test market demand and the technical feasibility of your solution simultaneously, before writing a single line of production code or finalizing your workflow.

Let's say your idea is to offer a service called "ResumeBot AI" that takes a user's LinkedIn profile URL and transforms it into a perfectly formatted PDF resume tailored for a specific job description. Building the front-end website, the payment processing, and the backend automation to do this reliably could take weeks or months. The Wizard of Oz approach is different. You would start by creating a simple landing page with a tool like Carrd or Webflow. The page would describe the service and have a simple form: "Paste your LinkedIn URL," "Paste the job description," and "Enter your email." You could even add a payment button using Stripe or PayPal to test willingness to pay, perhaps charging a small fee like $10 for the service.

When a customer fills out the form and pays, you get an email notification. Now, you become the "wizard." You manually go to their LinkedIn profile, copy the information, and paste it into one of the AI content generation tools you shortlisted in Chapter 2. You use a prompt like, "Rewrite this LinkedIn profile as a professional resume, emphasizing the skills relevant to the following job description..." You take the AI's output, paste it into a Google Doc, clean up the formatting, make any necessary edits for quality, and export it as a PDF. Then, you email the finished PDF to the customer with a message like, "Here is your resume, generated by ResumeBot AI!"

From the customer's perspective, they experienced a seamless, magical AI service. From your perspective, you just conducted an incredibly valuable experiment. You learned several things: 1) Are people willing to pay for this solution? (Did anyone click the 'buy' button?) 2) Can the AI tool actually produce a quality output from the given inputs? (How much editing did it require?) 3) How long does the entire "manual-automation" process take? (Is this scalable?) This method allows you to validate the most critical business assumptions with minimal upfront investment, giving you real-world feedback from paying customers from day one.

A Practical Walk-through: Testing the AI Meeting Summarizer

Let's get practical and walk through an experiment, step-by-step, using the idea of an "AI agent that attends Zoom meetings and automatically generates action items." In Chapter 2, you would have shortlisted a few tools from the "AI Agents and Workflow Automation Platforms" category, perhaps tools like FuseBase or others that can handle transcription and AI analysis. Now it's time to test them.

Step 1: Establish the Baseline. Before you test the AI, you need to understand the current reality. This is your control group. Find or record a ten-minute video of a project team meeting. Now, start a stopwatch and perform the task manually. Listen to the recording and transcribe it. Then, review the transcript and pull out all the specific action items, who is responsible, and any deadlines mentioned. Stop the clock. Let's say this manual process took you 25 minutes. You now have a "ground truth" list of action items and a baseline time to beat. This manual work is tedious, but it is the most important part of the experiment. Without a baseline, you have no way to measure improvement.

Step 2: Prepare the Experiment. Log into the free trial of Tool A. Upload the same ten-minute meeting recording. Configure the tool according to its documentation, telling it that your goal is to get a transcript and a summary of action items. This setup process is part of the experiment; if it takes you two hours just to figure out the interface, that's an important data point about the tool's ease of use.

Step 3: Run the Test and Gather the Output. Click the "run" button and let the AI do its work. Time how long it takes for the platform to process the file and produce the output. Once it's done, you will have an AI-generated transcript and, hopefully, a list of action items. This is your raw experimental output.

Step 4: Measure, Analyze, and Compare. Now you put on your analyst hat and compare the AI's output to your manual baseline using a simple scorecard.

First, track the Time Saved. The manual process took 25 minutes. The AI process might have taken 1 minute to upload and run, and then another 5 minutes for you to review and make minor edits to its output. The total time for the AI-assisted process is 6 minutes. The time saved is 19 minutes, a 76% reduction. This is a powerful metric that speaks directly to your value proposition.

Next, assess Accuracy. Compare the AI's list of action items to your "ground truth" list. Let's say your manual list had 10 action items. The AI identified 8 of them correctly, missed one entirely, and hallucinated one that wasn't actually mentioned. You could score its accuracy as 8/10, or 80%. Is 80% good enough for your service? Maybe. It depends on the criticality of the missed items. This quantitative measure is far more useful than saying the tool "mostly worked."

Then, evaluate the Output Quality. This is more subjective but equally important. Read the AI-generated summary. Is it coherent? Is the language professional? Does it capture the nuances of the conversation? You might rate the quality on a simple 1-5 scale, where 1 is "unusable garbage" and 5 is "perfect, client-ready output." This helps you distinguish between a tool that is technically accurate but produces robotic, clunky text, and one that generates natural, useful prose.

Finally, consider the Cost. The free trial won't last forever. Check the tool's pricing page. If they charge based on transcription minutes, calculate the cost for this ten-minute test. If it cost $0.50 to process this meeting, you can now start to model the unit economics of your business. If you plan to charge clients $10 per summarized meeting, a $0.50 cost gives you a healthy margin. If the tool costs $5 to process the meeting, your business model is likely not viable.

Repeat this entire process for Tool B and Tool C. At the end of this exercise, you will have a comparison table with hard data on time savings, accuracy, quality, and cost for each of your shortlisted tools. The vague notion of "a meeting summarizer" has been transformed into a data-driven business case.

Validating Market Interest Before You Build

So far, we've focused on testing technical feasibility: can the AI do the job? But there's another, equally critical question: does anyone care? You can build the most accurate, efficient AI tool in the world, but if it solves a problem nobody has or is willing to pay for, your business is destined to fail. Therefore, another type of rapid experiment is needed, one that tests the market, not just the machine.

Let's return to the niche idea of providing AI-generated social media content for independent coffee shops. You've already run a technical experiment and found a tool like Jasper can produce decent-quality Instagram captions from simple prompts. You know the tech can work. Now you need to know if the market wants it.

The goal of this experiment is: "Can I generate demonstrable interest from coffee shop owners for an AI-powered social media content service?" Your input will be ten sample Instagram posts you've created with the AI tool, complete with AI-generated images. Your output will be measured in customer engagement.

Here's how you could run this market validation test with a budget of less than $100. First, use a simple website builder to create a one-page "coming soon" site. The headline might read: "Effortless Social Media for Your Coffee Shop. Get 10 Free AI-Generated Posts." Display your best sample posts on the page. Add a simple email sign-up form that says, "Join the wait list to claim your free posts."

Next, go to a platform like Facebook or Instagram, where you can run highly targeted ads. Create a small ad campaign with a budget of $50. Target the ad specifically to people whose job title is "Owner" or "Manager" and whose business interest is "Coffee Shops," within a specific geographic area. The ad will feature one of your best AI-generated images and text, with a link back to your landing page.

For the next week, you do nothing but watch the numbers. How many people clicked on your ad? This is your click-through rate (CTR). Of those who landed on your page, how many signed up for the wait list? This is your conversion rate. Did you get any emails or direct messages asking for more information or pricing? These are your qualitative signals of interest.

After a week, you analyze the results. If you spent $50 and got 30 coffee shop owners to sign up for your wait list, that is an incredibly strong signal. You have validated that the problem is real and your proposed solution is attractive. You have a list of warm leads to talk to for customer interviews and to be your first beta testers. If, however, you spend $50 and get zero signups, that is also a valuable, if disappointing, result. It tells you that something is wrong. Perhaps your messaging was off, your sample posts weren't compelling, or, most critically, that coffee shop owners simply don't see this as an urgent enough problem to even click a button for a free solution. This information, discovered in one week for $50, is infinitely more valuable than finding it out after six months of building a product nobody wants.

These experiments, both technical and market-facing, are not one-time events. They are the building blocks of an iterative cycle: Build a small thing, test it, measure the results, and learn from them. What you learned from one experiment should inform the design of the next. Perhaps your first test showed that the AI was bad at extracting deadlines from meetings. Your next experiment could be to test a different AI tool that specializes in that specific task, or to tweak your prompt to be more explicit in asking for deadlines. Each cycle gets you closer to a solution that is both technically viable and commercially desirable. You have moved beyond mere ideas and are now generating real-world data, building your business on a foundation of evidence, not assumptions. With this validated learning in hand, you are now ready to take the next step: building your first real prototype.

* * *

4

Case Study: Building with FuseBase Portal

Theory, as the old saying goes, can only take you so far. We have spent the last three chapters laying a critical foundation: identifying a high-value problem, surveying the landscape of available AI tools, and learning how to run lean, data-driven experiments to test our core assumptions. We have moved from a vague idea to a validated concept backed by evidence. Now, it is time to take the next logical step. It is time to stop testing components in isolation and start assembling them into a functional, cohesive whole. It is time to build our first real prototype.

This chapter shifts from abstract principles to concrete practice. We will walk through a detailed case study, building a minimum viable product for a fictional AI-powered business from the ground up. The purpose is to demystify the process and show you, step-by-step, how the concepts we've discussed translate into clicks, configurations, and tangible results. By following along, you will see how a no-code platform can be used to construct a sophisticated, branded, and valuable service in a matter of hours, not months. This isn't about writing code; it's about strategic assembly.

For this case study, we will use FuseBase as our primary platform. We've chosen it because it elegantly combines several key features that are often required for service-based AI businesses: branded client-facing portals, internal knowledge bases, and trainable AI agents that can interact with that knowledge. This combination allows an entrepreneur to build a complete, professional client experience within a single ecosystem. While we are using one specific tool for this example, the principles and the process, defining a goal, structuring the workspace, training the AI, and measuring the impact, are universal and can be applied to any set of tools you choose for your own venture.

Setting the Scene: The Inefficient On-boarding Problem

Let's introduce our fictional startup: "ClientFlow AI." The founder, a former management consultant named Alex, has identified a niche based on a problem she experienced firsthand. Small consulting firms, creative agencies, and freelance professionals are often brilliant at their core service but chaotic in their client administration. Specifically, their client on-boarding process is a mess. It's a scattered flurry of emails, attachments, follow-up reminders, and repetitive questions that consumes valuable billable hours and starts the client relationship on a disorganized, unprofessional footing.

The problem is clear and urgent. For the consultant, it's a time-consuming, non-billable activity that distracts from the actual paid work. For the client, it's a confusing and frustrating experience that creates a poor first impression and erodes confidence before the project has even begun. Alex has validated this problem through interviews, as discussed in Chapter 1, and knows that consultancies are willing to pay to solve it.

The proposed solution is ClientFlow AI, a service that provides small consultancies with a streamlined, automated, and professionally branded on-boarding portal for each new client. Instead of a messy email chain, the client gets a single, secure link to a centralized hub. This portal will automate document collection, use a custom-trained AI agent to provide instant answers to common questions, and offer a clear, visible tracker for all on-boarding tasks.

Our goal for this chapter is to build the first functional prototype of the ClientFlow AI portal for a hypothetical consulting client, Innovate Corp. We will use FuseBase to create this entire experience, transforming a collection of ideas and experimental results into something we can actually show and test with a potential customer.

Step 1: Laying the Foundation, The Branded Workspace

The first step in creating a professional service is to look the part. A client's first interaction with your solution sets the tone for the entire relationship. A generic, unstyled interface screams "amateur," while a clean, branded experience inspires confidence and justifies the price you're charging. Before we add any content or AI smarts, we will create the digital "building" where our client will be welcomed.

Inside FuseBase, the top-level container is called a "Workspace." We begin by creating a new workspace and giving it the name of our client: "Innovate Corp On-boarding." This immediately establishes a dedicated, private environment. The next crucial action is to apply the branding of our service, ClientFlow AI. This is a simple but high-impact process. We navigate to the workspace settings and upload the ClientFlow AI logo. We then select a brand color, specific shade of blue from the logo, to be used for buttons, links, and highlights throughout the portal.

Finally, and perhaps most importantly, we configure a custom domain. Instead of sending the client a generic link like fusebase.com/workspace/xyz123, we set it up so the portal is accessible at innovatecorp.clientflow.ai. This small change has a profound psychological effect. From the client's perspective, this isn't some third-party tool they've been invited to; it is a secure, proprietary platform provided by the consultancy they just hired.

In less than fifteen minutes, we have created a professional, secure, and fully branded shell. This isn't just window dressing. It's a fundamental part of the value proposition. We are selling a service that makes our customers, the consultants, look good to their customers. The branded portal is the tangible proof of that promise. With this foundation in place, we can now start building the functional rooms inside our digital office.

Step 2: Building the Scaffolding, Structuring the Portal

With the branded workspace ready, we need to give it structure. An empty portal is as useless as an empty office. We need to create a logical, intuitive layout that guides the new client through the on-boarding process. The goal is to anticipate their needs and lay out a clear path, eliminating the confusion that defines the typical email-based on-boarding experience. Using FuseBase's page and nesting capabilities, we'll build out the essential sections of the portal.

First, we create a top-level page and title it "START HERE: Welcome to Innovate Corp." This page will serve as the client's landing spot. On this page, we don't just write text; we embed a short, personalized welcome video. This could be a simple recording from the lead consultant, greeting the client by name and giving a 60-second overview of the portal. This human touch is critical for building rapport and encouraging adoption. Below the video, we include a simple checklist of the three main on-boarding steps they need to complete.

Next, we create the core functional sections of the portal as separate pages, which will appear in a clean navigation menu on the left side of the screen.

The first section is "1. Required Documents." The old way involved emailing files back and forth, leading to version control issues and lost attachments.

The new way is a dedicated page with clear instructions. We create sub-pages or "upload blocks" for each required item: "Signed Master Services Agreement (MSA)," "Initial Project Questionnaire," and "Brand Style Guide." The client can simply drag and drop their files into the designated areas. This centralizes everything, providing a single source of truth for both the client and the consultant.

The second section is "2. On-boarding Task Tracker." Transparency is key to a good client relationship. Here, we use a simple table or a Kanban-style board to list the key on-boarding milestones. Each item has a status (e.g., Not Started, In Progress, Complete) and an owner (e.g., Innovate Corp, Consultant). Sample tasks might include "Submit Required Documents," "Schedule Kick-Off Call," and "Provide Access to Analytics." This visual tracker eliminates the need for "just checking in" emails and gives both parties a shared, real-time view of progress.

The final, and most important, section for our AI is "3. Project Knowledge Base." This section is initially for the client's reference but will soon become the brain of our AI assistant. We create a few key documents within it, pre-empting the client's most common questions.

With these sections in place, our portal is no longer just a branded shell; it is a structured, functional tool. We have thoughtfully designed the flow of information, replacing the chaos of an inbox with the clarity of a purpose-built system. The stage is now set for our star performer: the AI agent.

Step 3: Breathing Life into the System, On-boarding the AI Agent

This is where the magic happens. We are now going to transform our static, well-organized portal into a dynamic, intelligent assistant. The AI agent in FuseBase works by ingesting and understanding the content you provide within a specific workspace. Its purpose is to answer questions and perform tasks based only on that curated information. This is a critical concept: we are not connecting to a generic, all-knowing AI. We are building a specialist, an expert whose entire world is the Innovate Corp on-boarding project. This constrained knowledge is what makes it safe, accurate, and incredibly useful.

The first step is to feed the agent its "textbooks." We revisit the "Project Knowledge Base" section we created in the previous step and start populating it with high-quality information. The quality of our input here will directly determine the quality of the AI's output. Garbage in, garbage out.

We create a comprehensive "Frequently Asked Questions (FAQ)" document. We draw on Alex's (our fictional founder) experience and the interviews she conducted to list the top 20 questions every new client asks. These include: "What are your business hours?", "Who is my main point of contact for billing questions?", "What is the standard response time for emails?", and "How do I schedule a meeting?" For each question, we write a clear, concise, and definitive answer.

Next, we upload key project documents into the knowledge base. This might include a sanitized version of the Master Services Agreement, the original Statement of Work (SOW) that outlines the project scope, and a document detailing the communication plan. These documents contain hundreds of potential answers to more specific questions a client might have later.

With the knowledge base populated, we are ready to activate the AI. In the workspace settings, we enable the AI Agent. We give it a name to make it feel more approachable, let's call it "Flow." We then provide it with a core instruction, a "prime directive" that governs its behavior. We configure its prompt to say: "You are Flow, the friendly and professional AI assistant for the Innovate Corp on-boarding process. Your sole purpose is to help the client find information and answer their questions based exclusively on the documents provided in the Project Knowledge Base. If you cannot find an answer in the provided documents, you must respond with 'I do not have that information, but I can notify your project manager. Would you like me to do that?' Do not invent answers."

This instruction is the agent's constitution. It prevents it from "hallucinating" or making up incorrect information, which is the biggest risk with general-purpose AIs. The agent now has a name, a library to study from, and a clear set of rules. It is time to send it to school. We run the "training" process, where FuseBase indexes all the content in the knowledge base, creating a specialized model that understands the relationships between the concepts in our documents.

Finally, we test our newly trained agent. We open the chat interface within the portal and start asking it questions, playing the role of the client.

"Who is my account manager?" The AI should correctly pull the name from the welcome
document.

"What is the deadline for the first deliverable?" It should find the relevant date in the SOW.

"What's the weather like in Toronto?" It should correctly respond, *"I do not have that*
information..." because the weather is not mentioned in our project documents.

After a few rounds of testing and tweaking the documents in our knowledge base, our AI agent, Flow, is ready for duty. It is now a 24/7 expert on the project, capable of instantly answering dozens of questions that would have previously resulted in an email and a delay.

Step 4: Measuring What Matters, Impact and Value

We have successfully built a functional prototype of the ClientFlow AI portal. It is branded, structured, and intelligent. But a prototype is only useful if it delivers measurable value. How do we know if our solution is actually better than the manual process it's designed to replace? We need to measure its impact against the key metrics of time, quality, and cost.

First, let's analyze Time Savings. This is the most potent value proposition for our target customer, the busy consultant. We can run a side-by-side comparison. The "Old Way" of on-boarding a client, with all the back-and-forth emails, document searches, and repetitive question-answering, might take a consultant a total of 4-5 hours of fragmented work over the first week. The "New Way," using our portal, requires about 30 minutes of initial setup (duplicating a template and personalizing the welcome message). After that, the system takes over. The client self-serves their document uploads and gets their questions answered by the AI. The time saved for the consultant is therefore massive, several hours per client. This is a number that immediately gets a potential customer's attention.

Next, we evaluate the Improvement in Client Experience. This is a qualitative metric, but no less important. The old process was defined by confusion and delay. The new process is defined by clarity and immediacy. The client has a single source of truth, a clear roadmap, and instant answers. We can measure this by including a one-question survey on the final on-boarding task: "On a scale of 1-10, how easy and clear was this on-boarding process?" Getting consistent scores of 9 or 10 provides powerful social proof and testimonials for our service.

Then, we consider Error Reduction. The old way was prone to human error. The wrong version of a file gets used, a key question in an email gets missed, or a task is forgotten. Our structured portal minimizes these risks. Document versioning is clear. The AI provides consistent answers every time. The task tracker ensures nothing falls through the cracks. This reduction in risk and rework is a hidden but significant financial benefit.

Finally, we can begin to model the Unit Economics. Let's assume the Fuse-Base platform costs ClientFlow AI a certain amount per client workspace per month. By calculating the immense time savings for the consultant (e.g., 4 hours saved at an average consulting rate of $150/hour = $600 of value), ClientFlow AI can confidently charge a subscription or a flat fee (e.g., $250 per on-boarded client) that provides a fantastic return on investment for the customer while leaving a healthy profit margin for the business. The prototype allows us to move these numbers from guesswork to a data-backed financial model.

Extracting the Guiding Principles

This case study was not just an academic exercise in using a particular piece of software. It was a practical demonstration of several core principles that are essential for building any successful AI-based business. By extracting these lessons, we can create a repeatable framework for future projects.

Principle 1: The Right Tool for the Integrated Job. We didn't choose FuseBase because it had the most features, but because it had the right combination of features for our specific problem. It integrated the client-facing portal, the knowledge management, and the AI agent into one system. This avoided the complexity of having to stitch together three separate tools. The lesson is to always map your complete workflow first, and then find a tool that mirrors that workflow as closely as possible.

Principle 2: An AI is a Reflection of its Library. The AI agent, Flow, was only as effective as the knowledge base we curated for it. The effort we put into writing a clear FAQ and uploading structured documents paid off directly in the quality and accuracy of its responses. The success of many AI service businesses lies not in the AI model itself, but in the quality and structure of the proprietary data used to train it. Your value is in the curriculum you design for the AI.

Principle 3: Design the Entire Experience. The ClientFlow AI prototype was more than just an automation. It was a complete, branded experience.

The custom domain, the logo, the welcome video, and the logical flow all worked together to create a feeling of professionalism and care. When building your own service, remember that you are not just selling a function; you are selling an outcome and an emotion. The user interface and the client journey are just as important as the backend technology.

Principle 4: Build to Test. This prototype, as complete as it seems, is not the final product. It is an artifact built for the express purpose of getting real-world feedback. The next step is to put this portal in front of a real pilot customer. We need to watch them use it. Where do they hesitate? What questions do they ask that the AI can't answer? What features do they ignore? This user feedback is the fuel for the next iteration. The goal is not to build something perfect in a vacuum, but to build something tangible that can be improved through direct interaction with the market.

By walking through this case study, we have bridged the critical gap between experimentation and execution. We have seen how a well-defined problem can be addressed with an off-the-shelf, no-code platform to create a valuable, professional, and marketable service. We now have a tangible asset, a working prototype that makes our business real. It is something we can demonstrate, test, and, most importantly, sell.

* * *

5

Identifying Your Ideal Customer

You have a working prototype. It's a tangible, functional thing, born from a validated problem and assembled with carefully chosen AI tools. You've seen it work, at least on your own desktop. It feels like you've reached the summit of a huge mountain. In reality, you've just made it to base camp. The real expedition, finding people who will actually pay for your creation, is about to begin. To find them, you need a map. Not a map of a country or a city, but a map of a person. You need a detailed, almost unnervingly specific portrait of your perfect customer.

Up to this point, your focus has been internal, centered on the problem and the technology. Now, we must pivot 180 degrees and look outward. The most sophisticated AI engine in the world is worthless if it's aimed at the wrong target. Building a product without an intimate understanding of who it's for is like writing a love letter addressed, "To Whom It May Concern." It's a message with no recipient, an engine with no driver. This chapter is about finding that recipient. It's about moving from a general understanding of a problem to a crystal-clear picture of the human being who feels that problem most acutely.

This process is not an optional marketing exercise to be done later. It is a core strategic activity that will inform every subsequent decision you make. The profile you create will dictate your marketing language, your pricing structure, your feature roadmap, and your sales strategy. It will tell you where to advertise, what to write in your emails, and what to prioritize in your next product update. Without this profile, you are operating blind, spending time and money on guesswork. With it, every action becomes more focused, more efficient, and infinitely more effective.

From "Anyone" to "Someone"

The single most common and deadly mistake a new founder can make is believing their product is for "everyone." The second most deadly is believing it is for a vaguely defined group like "small businesses" or "busy professionals." These are not customer segments; they are oceans. Your fledgling business cannot afford to boil the ocean. You need to find a small, accessible pond where you can be the biggest fish. Identifying your Ideal Customer Profile (ICP) is the process of finding that pond.

Think of the ClientFlow AI service we prototyped in the last chapter. Its purpose is to streamline client onboarding. Who is it for? A novice founder might say, "It's for any business that has clients!" This is technically true but practically useless. A giant corporation like Deloitte has clients, and so does a solo freelance wedding photographer. Their needs, budgets, buying processes, and pain points are so wildly different that they might as well be on different planets. Trying to build and market a single solution for both is a recipe for failure. The product will be too complex for the photographer and too simple for Deloitte. The marketing message will be too corporate for one and too casual for the other.

The power of a focused customer profile lies in the magic of resonance. When your marketing message speaks directly to a specific person's specific problem in the language they use, it cuts through the noise. A wedding photographer scrolling through Instagram might ignore an ad for "Client

Process Automation Software," but they will stop dead in their tracks for an ad that says, "Stop Chasing Brides for Contracts and Questionnaires. Onboard Your Couples in One Click." The second message resonates because it is aimed at someone not "anyone." It demonstrates a deep understanding of their world. To achieve that level of specificity, you need to build a formal profile.

The Two Halves of the Coin: ICP and Persona

In the world of customer profiling, you'll frequently encounter two terms: Ideal Customer Profile (ICP) and Buyer Persona. They are often used interchangeably, but they represent two distinct, complementary concepts, especially in a B2B context. An ICP defines the perfect company to sell to, while a Buyer Persona defines the perfect person within that company to sell to. If you are selling directly to consumers (B2C), your focus will be almost entirely on the persona. But if you sell to other businesses, you need both.

An Ideal Customer Profile (ICP) is a description of the firm that is a perfect fit for your solution. It's defined by firmographics, the organizational equivalent of demographics. Think of it as a set of filters you would apply to a database of every company in the world to find your most likely buyers. For our ClientFlow AI service, the ICP is not "businesses." It's "Boutique consulting firms and creative agencies with 5 to 50 employees, located in North America, that generate over $500,000 in annual revenue and currently use email and spreadsheets to manage their client intake." Each of those qualifiers, company size, industry, location, revenue, current tech stack is a firmographic filter that dramatically narrows the field and increases the probability of a sale.

A Buyer Persona is a semi-fictional representation of the actual human being you need to influence. Even in a B2B sale, you are not selling to a building or a logo; you are selling to a person. The persona brings that person to life with demographic details, but more importantly, with psychographic insights into their goals, challenges, and daily life. Within our ideal consulting firm, who is the person feeling the pain of messy onboarding the most? Is it "Patricia the Project Manager," who is 35, overwhelmed by administrative tasks, and whose primary goal is to deliver projects on time without working 60-hour weeks? Or is it "Charles the CEO," who is 55, frustrated by client complaints about disorganization, and whose primary goal is to increase the firm's profitability and reputation? You might need to market to Patricia, but Charles is the one who signs the check. Understanding both is critical.

Building Your ICP: The Firmographic Blueprint

If you are a B2B business, defining your ICP is the first order of business. It's a strategic choice that defines your entire market. Your goal is to find the segment of the market where the problem you solve is most acute and the companies have the means and motivation to pay for it. A strong ICP is built on a foundation of clear, data-driven attributes.

Start with the Industry. Be specific. "Technology" is too broad. "Venture-backed SaaS companies in the FinTech space" is better. Different industries have different regulations, sales cycles, and jargon. Your AI solution, and the marketing for it, will be far more effective if it is tailored to a specific vertical. An AI deposition summarizer for law firms uses different language and solves a different compliance headache than an AI marketing copy generator for e-commerce brands.

Next, consider Company Size. This can be measured by annual revenue or number of employees. This is a critical factor because it is a strong proxy for budget, organizational complexity, and the types of problems a company faces. A 10-person company has different growing pains than a 500-person company. The former might need a simple, all-in-one tool, while the latter needs something that integrates with their existing enterprise software. Choose a size range that aligns with the price and complexity of your solution.

Geography is another important filter. Are you targeting local businesses, a specific country, or a global market? This has implications for language, currency, data privacy regulations (like GDPR in Europe), and support hours. For a new startup, it's often wise to start with a single geographic market, like the United States, before trying to tackle global complexities.

One of the most powerful but often overlooked firmographics for an AI business is the company's existing Technology Stack. What software do they already use? A company that has already invested in a CRM like Salesforce or a project management tool like Asana has demonstrated a willingness to pay for software and an understanding of its value. Furthermore, if your AI tool can integrate with the tools they already use, your value proposition becomes exponentially stronger. Marketing a meeting summarizer is one thing. Marketing an AI that automatically summarizes your Zoom meetings and puts the action items directly into your team's Asana project is a far more compelling proposition.

Finally, look for Trigger Events. Is there a specific event that makes a company suddenly need your solution? This could be a round of funding, a key executive hire (like a new Head of Sales), rapid hiring, or expansion into a new market. These events often create the "hair-on-fire" problems that send people actively searching for a solution like yours. Identifying these triggers gives you a powerful signal for when to reach out.

Bringing Your Persona to Life: Beyond the Job Title

Once you know the type of company you're targeting, you need to under-stand the people inside it. A persona is not just a job title. It's a deep dive into the psychology of your buyer. You are trying to understand their world so you can speak to them in a way that makes them feel seen, heard, and understood.

Start with basic Demographics. What is their job title? "Director of

Marketing," "Solo Founder," "Office Manager." How senior are they? This impacts their decision-making power. What is their approximate age or career stage? This can influence their tech-savviness and communication preferences.

Then, go deeper with Psychographics. This is where the persona truly comes to life.

Goals & Motivations: What are they trying to achieve in their role? What does success look like for them? Is it getting a promotion? Is it reducing stress? Is it making their team more effective? A project manager's goal isn't just to complete projects; it's to look competent and organized in front of her boss and clients.

Challenges & Frustrations: This is the flip side of their goals. What stands in their way? What tasks are a constant source of frustration? What part of their job do they dread? Our "Patricia the Project Manager" is frustrated by the endless manual follow-up and the mental load of tracking dozens of disconnected email threads. These are the specific pain points your AI solution should address.

A Day in the Life: Try to map out their daily routine. What are the first things they do when they get to work? What meetings do they attend? What software do they have open on their screen all day? This context helps you understand when and how your solution fits into their existing workflow.

Finally, you need to understand their Buying Behavior. How do they learn about new tools? Do they read industry blogs, listen to podcasts, or ask for recommendations in a private Slack community? Who do they need to get approval from to make a purchase? In a B2B sale, you often have multiple personas to consider: the User (the person who will use your tool every day, like Patricia), the Champion (the person who advocates for its adoption), the Economic Buyer (the person with the budget, like Charles the CEO), and sometimes even a Technical Buyer (someone from IT who needs to vet its security). Your marketing and sales process may need to address the distinct needs of each of these individuals.

The "Jobs to Be Done" Framework: A Shift in Perspective

Firmographics and personas are powerful, but they describe who the customer is, not why they buy. The "Jobs to Be Done" (JTBD) framework offers a profound shift in perspective. It posits that customers don't really "buy" products; they "hire" them to do a specific job. This simple idea can radically clarify your thinking about what your product is truly for.

The classic example, popularized by the late Clayton Christensen, involves a fast-food chain trying to sell more milkshakes. They surveyed customers, asking them what would make the milkshake better, should it be more chocolate, cheaper, thicker? They implemented the feedback, and nothing changed. Finally, a researcher stood in a store all day and just observed who was buying milkshakes. He discovered that a huge number of milkshakes were sold before 9 a.m. to people who were by themselves and got back into their cars and drove away.

When he interviewed these customers, he didn't ask about the milkshake. He asked, "What job were you trying to get done that led you to come here and order this milkshake?" It turned out the customers had a long, boring commute to work. They needed something that would keep them engaged and stave off hunger until lunchtime. They had tried other things for this job. A banana was gone too quickly. A bagel was dry and created crumbs. A donut left their fingers sticky. The milkshake was perfect for the job. It took a long time to drink through a thin straw, it filled them up, and it fit in the car's cup holder. The milkshake's real competitors weren't other milkshakes; they were bananas, bagels, and boredom.

When you apply this to your AI business, it forces you to look beyond the features of your product and focus on the customer's underlying motivation. The consultant using ClientFlow AI isn't just hiring it for the functional job of "collecting documents." They are hiring it for the emotional job of "reducing the anxiety of starting a new project" and the social job of "appearing professional and hyper-organized to a new client."

You can capture these insights using a "job story" format:
When _____ [situation], I want to _____ [motivation], so I can _____ [expected
outcome].

For ClientFlow AI, a job story might be:
When I sign a new client, I want to automate the administrative setup, so I can
focus my energy on the strategic work they're actually paying me for.

Notice this story contains no mention of AI, portals, or any specific technology. It's all about the user's context and desired outcome. Framing your value proposition in terms of the job you do for your customer is far more powerful than listing a set of features.

Creating Your Customer Profile Canvas

Now it's time to pull all these pieces together into a single, actionable document. A one-page Customer Profile Canvas prevents these insights from being scattered across different documents and makes them easy for your entire team to reference. This canvas becomes your north star for all customer-facing activities. You can create this as a simple document or a shared spreadsheet.

Here is a sample structure you can use, combining the ICP, Persona, and JTBD frameworks into one comprehensive view.

ClientFlow AI - Ideal Customer Profile: "The Modern Consultancy"

Section	Details
ICP (The Company)	**Industry:** Management Consulting, Marketing Agencies, B2B Service Providers.
	Company Size: 5-50 employees.
	Annual Revenue: $500k - $10M.
	Tech Stack: Uses Google Workspace/Office 365, Slack, and a modern project management tool (Asana, Trello, ClickUp). No existing dedicated onboarding software.
	Pain Signal: Job postings mention "managing multiple client projects" or "improving operational efficiency."
Primary Persona (The Human)	**Name & Role:** "Patricia the Project Manager" or "Alex the Account Director".
	Demographics: Age 30-45. Tech-savvy. Responsible for client success and project delivery.
	Goals: Deliver projects on time and on budget. Increase client satisfaction scores. Reduce personal administrative workload and stress.
	Frustrations: Chasing clients for information. Replying to the same questions over and over. Lack of a central place for project information. Feeling disorganized.
Jobs to Be Done (The Why)	**Functional Job:** Systematize the collection of client information and initial project assets.
	Emotional Job: Reduce the anxiety and mental clutter associated with starting a new project. Feel in control and professional.
	Social Job: Impress the new client with a smooth, modern, and organized on-boarding experience.
Watering Holes (The Where)	**Blogs/Publications:** Reads Harvard Business Review, industry-specific marketing or consulting blogs.
	Social Media: Active on LinkedIn. Member of professional groups related to project management or their specific industry.
	Communities: May be part of private Slack or Discord communities for agency owners or consultants.

The Hunt for Data

This canvas is a powerful tool, but it's only as valuable as the data used to create it. It must be built on research, not imagination. So, where do you get this information? You've actually already started.

The interviews you conducted back in Chapter 1 to validate the problem are your first source. Go back to those notes. This time, you're not just looking for pain points; you're looking for the language people used, the goals they mentioned, and the frustrations they expressed. If you can, conduct a second round of interviews. This time, your questions will be more targeted: "Can you walk me through what happened the last time you signed a new client?", "What other tools do you use every day?", "How do you currently share files and updates with clients?".

If you have pilot users from your prototype testing, they are a goldmine of information. They are your ICP incarnate. Talk to them. Observe them. Analyze how they use your tool. Their behavior is more truthful than their words.

LinkedIn is an incredible research tool for B2B personas. You can find people with the exact job title at the exact type of company in your ICP. Look at their profiles. What skills do they list? What groups are they members of? What content do they share? This gives you a direct window into their professional world.

And don't forget the "digital eavesdropping" from Chapter 1. Go back to those Reddit forums, Quora questions, and Facebook groups. But now, you're not just looking for problems; you're looking for persona details. Pay attention to the way people describe their jobs, their bosses, and their daily struggles. Every post is a potential insight that can be used to flesh out your canvas.

This detailed, well-researched customer profile is the final piece of your business foundation. You started with a problem, found the tools to build a solution, and prototyped a viable product. Now you know exactly who that product is for. You have your target. The next step is to decide on the precise business model you will use to sell it to them.

* * *

6

Choosing Your Business Model: B2B, B2C, or B2B2C

You've identified a problem, explored the AI tools to solve it, built a working prototype, and created a detailed profile of your ideal customer. Each step has brought your business into sharper focus. Now, you stand at a crucial fork in the road. You know who you are serving, but you must decide how you will serve them. This decision is about your business model, the fundamental architecture of how you create, deliver, and capture value. It dictates the entire shape of your company, from how you make your first dollar to how you build your team.

This is not a question of choosing a pricing strategy, which we will cover in a later chapter. Pricing is about how much you charge; your business model is about who you charge. Is your customer a company, an individual, or a company that serves an individual? The answer to this question will determine whether you embark on the path of Business-to-Business (B2B), Business-to-Consumer (B2C), or the complex hybrid of Business-to-Business-to-Consumer (B2B2C).

This choice is a direct and unavoidable consequence of the work you did in the previous chapter. The Ideal Customer Profile you painstakingly developed is not just an academic exercise; it is the primary input for this decision. Trying to select a business model without a clear customer in mind is like trying to choose an outfit without knowing if you're going to a wedding or a mud run. The context is everything. Each model comes with its own distinct set of rules, expectations, challenges, and rewards. Let's dissect them one by one so you can make an informed choice that aligns perfectly with the business you intend to build.

The B2B Path: Selling to Businesses

The Business-to-Business (B2B) model is perhaps the most straightforward and common path for AI-based startups, especially those born from solving a professional pain point. In a B2B model, your company sells its product or service directly to another company. The buyer is an organization, and your AI solution is designed to help that organization save money, make more money, improve its efficiency, or reduce its risk. The ClientFlow AI service we prototyped in Chapter 4 is a textbook B2B offering. Its customer is a consulting firm, and its purpose is to solve a business process problem.

If your Ideal Customer Profile from Chapter 5 was a firmographic sketch of a company, defined by its industry, employee count, and revenue, you are almost certainly building a B2B business. The core of this model is solving problems that have a clear, measurable impact on a company's bottom line. Because of this, the dynamics of a B2B sale are profoundly different from selling to an individual.

The most attractive feature of the B2B model is the potential for a significantly higher ticket price. Businesses have budgets. They are accustomed to paying for software and services that provide a clear return on investment (ROI). An individual might hesitate to spend $20 a month on an app, but a company won't blink at spending $500 a month on a solution that saves an employee ten hours of work. If that employee costs the company $50 an hour, the $500 software just provided a 100% return in a single month. This ability to frame your price in the context of tangible business value allows for much larger contract sizes. B2B pricing is often structured as a monthly or annual subscription, frequently on a per-user basis, which creates a predictable, recurring revenue stream.

However, this higher price point comes with a trade-off: a longer and more complex sales cycle. In a B2C transaction, the buyer and the user are usually the same person, and the decision can be made in minutes. In a B2B transaction, you are navigating an organization. The person who feels the pain (the user) might not be the person who has the authority to buy (the manager or executive) or the person who controls the budget (the finance department). You may also have to get security approval from the IT department. This means a single sale can involve multiple meetings, product demonstrations, proposals, contract negotiations, and security reviews. A typical B2B sales cycle can last anywhere from a few weeks to several months. Patience and process are paramount.

Another defining characteristic of the B2B world is the need for deeper integration. Your AI solution will not exist in a vacuum. It must fit into the customer's existing ecosystem of software. Our ClientFlow AI service becomes exponentially more valuable if it can automatically send uploaded documents to the company's Google Drive, create tasks in their Asana project, and send notifications to their team's Slack channel. This means that a robust and well-documented API (Application Programming Interface) is not a "nice-to-have"; it is a core requirement for many B2B products. Your ability to connect to the tools your customers already use is a major selling point.

Because of the complexity and high value of the sale, B2B is inherently relationship-driven. You can't acquire a $10,000-a-year customer with a clever Instagram ad. You acquire them by building trust and demonstrating expertise. Your marketing will focus on establishing your company as an authority in its niche. This involves creating in-depth content like white papers, case studies of successful customers, and webinars that educate your target audience. The sales process is consultative; it's about understanding a potential customer's specific problems and clearly articulating how your solution can solve them.

So, when is the B2B path right for you? It is the natural choice if the problem you identified is a business process, the pain is felt by employees in their professional capacity, and the value of your solution can be measured in business terms like time saved, revenue gained, or costs cut. If your passion lies in solving complex operational puzzles and building deep, lasting relationships with a smaller number of high-value clients, then the B2B model is your arena.

The B2C Path: Selling to Consumers

The Business-to-Consumer (B2C) model is what most people think of when they imagine a popular app or website. In a B2C model, you sell your AI-powered product or service directly to individual people for their personal use. The motivation for purchase is not ROI, but personal benefit: entertainment, convenience, education, self-improvement, or social connection. An AI app that generates personalized bedtime stories for children, a tool that helps users plan their vacation itineraries, or a service that creates custom-tailored diet plans are all examples of B2C AI businesses.

If your buyer persona from Chapter 5 was defined by personal demographics, interests, and life goals rather than a job title, you are on the B2C path. Here, you are not selling to an organization; you are selling to a vast and diverse public. The dynamics are a mirror image of the B2B world. Instead of a small number of large sales, your success depends on a large number of small sales.

The most significant advantage of the B2C model is the speed and simplicity of the sales cycle. The decision-maker is a single individual. There are no committees, no procurement departments, and no budget meetings. A customer can see an ad on TikTok, click through to your website or app store page, and make a purchase in under a minute. This creates the potential for rapid, explosive growth if your product strikes a chord with the market. The barrier to getting started is extremely low for the customer.

This accessibility necessitates a much lower price point. Consumers are inherently more price-sensitive than businesses. A B2C AI product is unlikely to command a $100 monthly subscription. Pricing is typically a small monthly fee (e.g., $5.99), a one-time purchase price, or a "freemium" model. In a freemium model, the core product is free to use, which helps it spread quickly, but users can pay to unlock advanced features, remove ads, or get more usage credits. Because the revenue per user is low, a B2C business must achieve significant scale to be profitable. You need thousands, if not millions, of users to build a substantial business.

To reach that scale, B2C marketing operates on a completely different plane than B2B. It is a game of mass communication. You cannot have a personal conversation with every potential user. Your marketing toolkit will include things like search engine optimization (SEO) to capture people searching for solutions, paid advertising on social media platforms like Facebook and Instagram, partnerships with influencers who can showcase your product to their audience, and public relations to get featured in popular blogs and magazines. The brand's voice and personality are critical. You are not just selling a utility; you are selling an identity and an experience.

The product itself must reflect this need for scale and simplicity. A B2C AI tool must be flawlessly intuitive from the moment it is opened. There is no manual, no training session, and no customer support specialist to walk a user through the setup. The on-boarding process must be self-explanatory and guide the user to their first "aha!" moment of value within seconds. If a user is confused or frustrated in the first minute, they will simply delete the app and never return. The user interface (UI) and user experience (UX) are not just important; they are the entire product.

The B2C model is the right choice if your AI solution addresses a problem or desire that millions of individuals share. If your passion is in creating simple, elegant, and delightful experiences that can touch a massive audience, and you are energized by the fast-paced world of consumer marketing, then the B2C path is for you. It's a high-stakes game of volume where user experience reigns supreme.

The Hybrid Path: The B2B2C Model

There exists a third, more intricate path that blends the other two: the Business-to-Business-to-Consumer (B2B2C) model. This is one of the most powerful but also one of the most challenging models to execute. In a B2B2C model, your company sells its AI-powered tool to another business (the first 'B'), which then incorporates it into their own product or service to serve their end customers (the 'C'). You are not the final brand the consumer interacts with; you are the "Intel Inside," the hidden technology that powers the experience.

A classic example would be an AI company that develops a sophisticated "virtual try-on" technology. They don't sell this technology directly to shoppers (that would be B2C). Instead, they sell it to an online fashion retailer like ASOS (the B2B part of the sale). ASOS then integrates this technology into its website, allowing its shoppers to see what a dress would look like on a model that matches their body type (the B2C part of the experience). Your company gets paid by ASOS, but your success is entirely dependent on whether ASOS's customers find the tool useful and engaging.

The defining characteristic of the B2B2C model is its combined complexity. You are effectively running two businesses at once. You must have a B2B sales and marketing motion to convince the business (the 'B') to adopt your technology. This involves all the hallmarks of a B2B sale: demos, ROI calculations, and contract negotiations. You need to convince ASOS that your virtual try-on tool will increase their sales and reduce their return rates.

Simultaneously, you must be obsessed with the end consumer's (the 'C') experience, even though they are not your direct customer. If the shoppers find your virtual try-on tool clunky, inaccurate, or slow, they won't use it. If they don't use it, it won't deliver the promised ROI to ASOS. And if it doesn't deliver ROI, ASOS will cancel their contract with you at the end of the year. This means your go-to-market strategy must address both audiences. You need to provide your business customer with a product that is not only powerful but also easy for them to implement and for their customers to love.

The value proposition must be crystal clear for both parties in the chain. The business customer needs to see a direct path to increased revenue or decreased costs. The end consumer needs to get a tangible benefit, like more confidence in their purchase, a more personalized experience, or a simpler way to accomplish a task. If the value proposition is weak for either party, the entire model collapses. The business won't buy it, or the consumer won't use it.

Choosing the B2B2C model makes sense when your AI solution is an enhancement or an enabler for another company's core business. It works when you can fundamentally improve the product or service that a business offers to its own customers. This model requires a deep understanding of the value chain of a specific industry. You need to see how you can insert your technology to create a win-win-win situation: a win for the consumer, a win for the business you sell to, and a win for your own company. It is a highly strategic play that can create deep, defensible moats around your business, but it demands a high level of operational excellence to manage the dual audiences.

Making Your Choice: The Strategic Alignment

With a clear understanding of these three models, the choice should now feel less like a wild guess and more like a logical conclusion. This decision is not about which model is "best" in a vacuum, but which model is the most authentic fit for the problem you solve, the customer you serve, and the value you create. To make your final decision, look back at the evidence you have already gathered.

First and foremost, examine your Ideal Customer Profile and Buyer Persona from Chapter 5. Who is the central character in the story of your business? Is it "Patricia the Project Manager," whose professional life is consumed by administrative chaos? That points directly to B2B. Is it "Dave the Dad," who wants a fun and educational new way to interact with his kids? That is unequivocally B2C. Is it "Susan the Salon Owner," who wants to offer her clients an AI-powered tool to see how a new hair color would look on them? That has the clear markings of a B2B2C play. Your customer profile is the most reliable compass you have.

Next, revisit the problem you defined in Chapter 1 and the value proposition that emerged from it. Is the value you provide measured in business metrics or personal ones? If your headline value proposition is "Cut your client on-boarding time by 80%," you are speaking the language of B2B. If it's "Never wonder what to cook for dinner again," you are speaking to a B2C audience. The language you naturally use to describe the benefit of your solution is a powerful indicator of your true model.

Finally, consider your own skills and passions as a founder. Are you excited by the idea of building relationships, crafting detailed proposals, and navigating corporate structures? That aligns well with the consultative nature of B2B sales. Are you energized by consumer psychology, brand building, and the potential for viral growth? That suggests a leaning toward B2C. Are you a strategic thinker who loves dissecting industries and forging partnerships? That mindset is essential for B2B2C. The model you choose will shape your daily activities for years to come, so it's wise to pick a path that plays to your strengths.

This decision is one of the most fundamental you will make as an entrepreneur. It sets the stage for everything that follows. Choosing B2B means you will soon be thinking about sales teams and integration partners. Choosing B2C means you will be focused on conversion rates and viral loops. Choosing B2B2C means you will be managing partner relationships and end-user feedback simultaneously. There is no right or wrong answer, only a right or wrong fit for the specific business you are building. By aligning your model with your customer and the problem you solve, you create a coherent strategy that gives you the best possible chance of success.

* * *

7

Naming & Branding Your AI Business

A powerful piece of technology that solves a real-world problem is a remarkable thing. But in a marketplace filled with remarkable things, it is not enough. Your solution needs an identity. It needs a name your customers can remember, a look they can recognize, and a personality they can connect with. This is the domain of naming and branding. It's the process of wrapping your technology in a story, transforming an abstract solution into a tangible entity that can build trust, communicate value, and stand out in an increasingly crowded field.

Many technically-minded founders view branding as a "soft," non-essential activity, something to be outsourced to a creative agency once the product is perfect and the revenue is flowing. This is a profound and costly mistake. Your name and brand are not decorative afterthoughts; they are strategic assets that begin working for you from day one. They are the handle your first customer uses to find you, the banner under which you build your reputation, and the primary vehicle for communicating who you are, what you do, and why it matters.

In the fast-evolving world of artificial intelligence, where new tools and platforms seem to launch daily, a strong brand is a crucial differentiator.

When two AI solutions offer similar features, customers will gravitate toward the one they trust, the one that feels more professional, and the one whose message resonates with their own goals. A great name can hint at your solution's benefit before a customer ever sees your product. A consistent brand identity creates a sense of reliability and professionalism, which is especially critical when you're asking businesses to trust your AI with their valuable data and workflows. This chapter is your guide to crafting that identity, from finding the perfect name to building the foundational elements of a brand that will serve you for years to come.

The Naming Framework: More Science Than Art

Choosing a name for your business can feel like a daunting creative challenge. The pressure to find something unique, catchy, and meaningful can lead to weeks of brainstorming, only to end in frustration. The key is to approach naming not as a mystical art form, but as a systematic process of generation and elimination. By applying a clear framework, you can move from a blank page to a shortlist of strong contenders in a structured and efficient way. A great name isn't found by a stroke of genius; it's engineered by applying a set of logical constraints.

The first and most important constraint is Clarity. For a new startup, especially in the B2B space, a name that clearly communicates what your business does is almost always superior to one that is merely clever or abstract. Your prospects are busy people. They will not take the time to solve a riddle to figure out your value proposition. A name like "Automated MeetingNotes.ai" leaves no doubt about the service offered. While it may not win any awards for poetry, it does the heavy lifting of qualifying your audience instantly. Someone who doesn't need automated meeting notes will ignore it, and someone who does will be immediately intrigued. This kind of self-evident clarity is a powerful marketing tool.

This doesn't mean your name must be boring. There is a spectrum between the purely descriptive and the wildly abstract. You can be evocative without being obscure. A name like "ClientFlow AI," which we used for our case study, isn't as blunt as "ClientOnboardingAutomation.com," but it still strongly suggests a benefit: making the client management process smoother and more fluid. The goal is to find the sweet spot where the name is intriguing but not confusing. When in doubt, always err on the side of clarity. You can build a creative brand around a clear name, but it's very difficult to clarify a confusing one.

The second principle is Simplicity. A name should be easy to say, easy to spell, and easy to remember. This sounds obvious, but it's a rule that is frequently broken in the tech world in a misguided attempt to appear unique. Avoid intentionally misspelled words (like "KlyentFlow"), awkward numbers, or hyphens. These gimmicks create friction. A customer who hears your name in a podcast should be able to type it into Google without having to guess at the spelling. A name that you have to spell out every time you say it over the phone is a name that is working against you. Read your potential names out loud. Are they smooth and phonetic, or are they a mouthful of clunky syllables? The simpler the name, the more easily it will spread through word-of-mouth.

The third and most unforgiving principle of modern naming is Availability. This is the great filter that eliminates most naming ideas in the 21st century. A name is only viable if you can own the digital real estate associated with it. Primarily, this means the ".com" domain name. While other extensions like ".ai" or ".io" are popular in the tech space, the ".com" is still the default in the minds of most customers. If the ".com" version of your name is taken by another business, especially one in a similar industry, you risk sending your customers directly to a competitor.

Before you fall in love with a name, your very first action should be to check its domain availability. Use a service like Namecheap, GoDaddy, or Google Domains to see if the ".com" is available for registration at a standard price.

If it is, you may have a winner. If it's taken or listed for sale for thousands of dollars, you should, in most cases, discard the name and move on. The same check should be performed for major social media handles. Is the name available on LinkedIn, X (formerly Twitter), and any other platform relevant to your business? Securing a consistent handle across all platforms is essential for building a clean and professional brand presence. A great name that is unavailable is not a great name; it's just a great idea for someone else's business.

Brainstorming Techniques and Name Categories

With the core principles of clarity, simplicity, and availability in mind, you can begin the creative process of generating ideas. Don't censor yourself at this stage; the goal is to create a long list of possibilities that you will filter later.

A great way to start is by brainstorming keywords related to your business. Think about your target customer, the problem you solve, the benefit you provide, and the technology you use. For our ClientFlow AI example, the keywords might include: client, customer, onboard, flow, streamline, automate, simple, path, guide, AI, agent, bot, nexus, portal, and so on. Once you have this list, you can start combining them or using them as seeds for more creative ideas.

Most business names fall into one of a few categories. Using these categories as prompts can help structure your brainstorming:

Descriptive Names: These names state exactly what the company does. They are great
   for SEO and clarity. Examples include MeetingSummarizer.ai,
   InvoiceScanner, or AITranscriptionService.com. The main
   drawback is that they can be generic and may limit your ability to expand into other
   services later.

Compound Names: These are created by combining two words. This is an extremely

popular and effective technique in tech. Think of FuseBase (Fuse + Base), Airtable (Air + Table), or Copy.ai (Copy + AI). You can

combine a word related to your function with a word that suggests a benefit or a

metaphor.

Evocative Names: These names use metaphor to suggest a benefit or feeling. They don't

describe the product literally but create a positive association. A name like "Zenith"

suggests reaching the peak of performance. "Loom" suggests weaving together different

video clips. These can be very powerful but require more marketing effort to connect the

name to the function.

Invented Names: These are completely made-up words. Think of "Google," "Zapier," or

"Asana." The advantage is that they are almost guaranteed to be unique and have an

available domain. The major disadvantage is that they have no inherent meaning. You

have to spend significant time and money to build that meaning into the minds of your

customers. For a bootstrapped startup, this is often a more difficult path.

Use these categories to play with your keyword list. Try combining them in different ways. Use a thesaurus to find interesting synonyms. Don't be afraid to generate dozens or even hundreds of possibilities. Quantity is your friend in the brainstorming phase.

The Validation Gauntlet: Putting Your Names to the Test

Once you have a long list of potential names, it's time to be ruthless. Your goal is to narrow this list down to a final three to five contenders that you will put through a final series of tests. This filtering process should be objective and systematic.

The first pass is the Availability Check we've already discussed. Go through your entire list and immediately eliminate any name where the ".com" domain and key social handles are not available. This will likely cut your list down by over 90%. This is good. It forces you to focus on the names that are actually viable.

The second pass is the Google Test. For each remaining name, type it into Google and see what comes up. Are there any other companies with the same or a very similar name? Even if they are in a different industry, it can create confusion. Does the name have any unintended negative connotations? Is it a slang term in another language? Does it rhyme with something unfortunate? A quick search can save you from future embarrassment.

The third pass is the "Say It Out Loud" Test. Say the name. Say it to a friend. Ask them to spell it back to you. Is it easy and intuitive? Does it sound professional? Some names look great on paper but are awkward to pronounce, which creates a barrier to word-of-mouth marketing.

After these initial filters, you should have a small shortlist of your strongest candidates. Now it's time for some external feedback. This doesn't need to be an expensive market research project. You can run a simple survey using a tool like Google Forms and send it to a dozen people who fit your ideal customer profile. Don't just ask, "Which name do you like best?" That invites subjective opinion. Instead, ask questions that test for clarity and resonance:

"Based on this name alone, what do you think this company does?"

"Which of these names sounds the most trustworthy?"

"Which of these names sounds like it would be the easiest to use?"

The answers to these questions will provide invaluable data. If everyone thinks your favorite name sounds like a video game company, but you're selling to law firms, you have a problem. The name that most consistently aligns with your intended function and brand attributes is likely your winner. After this final step, you should have enough confidence to make a decision, register the domain, and secure the social handles immediately.

Beyond the Name: Building Your Core Brand Identity

The name is the anchor of your brand, but it is not the entire ship. Your brand is the sum of every interaction a customer has with your company. It's the feeling they get when they visit your website, the tone of the emails you send, and the promise you implicitly make with your service. Building a brand is about intentionally shaping that perception. For a new startup, you don't need a hundred-page brand style guide, but you do need to define and consistently apply a few core elements.

The first element is your Visual Identity. This primarily consists of your logo and your color palette. Again, do not over complicate this at the start. Your goal is a clean, professional logo that looks good in a browser tab and on a LinkedIn page. You do not need to spend thousands of dollars on a custom design from a top agency. Services like Fiverr or Upwork can connect you with designers who can create a perfectly adequate logo for a very reasonable price. Alternatively, tools like Canva have logo makers that allow you to create something simple yourself.

When designing your logo and choosing your brand colors, think about the personality you want to convey. Are you building a brand that is serious, secure, and trustworthy? You might lean toward a palette of blues, grays, and clean, strong fonts. Are you building a brand that is creative, fun, and innovative? You might choose brighter colors and a more playful font. The key is to choose a direction and stick with it. Your logo, website colors, and marketing materials should all use the same visual language. This consistency is what builds recognition and a sense of professionalism.

The second, and arguably more important, element is your Brand Voice and Tone. How do you sound when you talk to your customers? This is one of the most powerful and overlooked aspects of branding. Your tone should be a direct reflection of your buyer persona. If you are selling to enterprise IT managers, your tone should be professional, technical, and authoritative. If you are selling to freelance artists, your tone can be more casual, creative, and inspirational.

Define a few keywords that describe your desired tone. For example: "Friendly, but not unprofessional. Confident, but not arrogant. Helpful, but not condescending." Write these down. This voice should be applied everywhere you write copy: on your website, in your email sequences, in your social media posts, and even in the error messages inside your application. It should also inform the way your AI agent communicates with users. A consistent voice makes your brand feel like a coherent personality, not just a faceless piece of software.

The final piece of your core brand identity is your Brand Promise. This is a simple, one-sentence statement that clearly articulates the value you deliver to your customers. It's the "why" behind your brand. For ClientFlow AI, the promise might be: "To make your consultancy look professional and save you hours of administrative work on every new project." This is not a marketing tagline that you put on a t-shirt. It's an internal guiding principle.

Your brand promise is the standard against which you should measure every decision. Does this new feature help us deliver on our promise? Does our pricing model reflect the value promised? Does our customer support experience live up to this promise? When your name, your visual identity, your brand voice, and your product all work together to deliver on a clear and consistent promise, you have built a strong brand. It becomes a self-reinforcing system where every element builds trust and clarifies your value in the mind of the customer.

* * *

8

Legal Considerations & Business Formation

We have arrived at the chapter that many creative entrepreneurs dread. It's the one filled with acronyms, paperwork, and conversations that feel far removed from the exciting work of building an innovative AI product. It can be tempting to treat the legal and administrative setup of your business as an afterthought, a box to be ticked later, once the "real work" is done. This is a dangerous and potentially catastrophic mistake. Getting your legal structure right from the very beginning is not bureaucratic busywork; it is the act of building a strong foundation for your entire enterprise.

Think of it this way: your business idea is the engine, and your AI prototype is the chassis, but your legal structure is the steel safety cage that protects you, the driver. Without it, the first bump in the road, a disagreement with a partner, a customer complaint, or an unexpected debt, could cause the entire vehicle to collapse, putting your personal assets at risk. This chapter is your guide to building that safety cage. It will demystify the essential choices and actions required to transform your project from a high-risk hobby into a legitimate, protected business entity.

The information here is designed to make you an informed founder; it will provide you with the foundational knowledge to understand the landscape and ask the right questions. However, it is not, and cannot be, a substitute for professional legal advice. The laws governing businesses are complex and vary significantly by location. One of the wisest investments you can make at this stage is to consult with a qualified attorney and an accountant who have experience with tech startups. This chapter will ensure you walk into that meeting prepared, confident, and ready to make the best decisions for your future company.

Choosing Your Business Entity: The Structural Blueprint

The first and most fundamental decision you will make is choosing the legal structure for your business. This choice will have long-term consequences for your personal liability, your tax obligations, and your ability to raise money in the future. While there are several options, most startups will choose from one of four common structures. Let's break down the pros and cons of each, specifically through the lens of an AI-based business.

The Default Settings: Sole Proprietorship and General Partnership

If you start working on a business by yourself without filing any official paperwork, you are, by default, a sole proprietor. If you start with one or more partners, you are a general partnership. These are the easiest and cheapest ways to start, as they require no formal action. However, this simplicity comes at an unacceptably high price: unlimited personal liability.

In these structures, there is no legal distinction between you and the business.

They are one and the same. This means that if your business incurs debt or is sued, your personal assets, your car, your house, your savings account, can be seized to satisfy those obligations. Given the nature of AI, where unforeseen issues with data, privacy, or algorithmic bias can create significant legal risks, operating as a sole proprietor or general partnership is like walking a tightrope without a net. It is not a recommended path for any serious technology venture.

The Modern Standard: The Limited Liability Company (LLC)

The Limited Liability Company (LLC) is a hybrid structure that has become incredibly popular for new businesses, and for good reason. It combines the primary benefit of a corporation, limited liability, with the flexibility and operational ease of a partnership or sole proprietorship. Creating an LLC establishes your business as a separate legal entity. This creates a "corporate veil," a legal wall between your business finances and your personal finances.

If an LLC is properly formed and maintained, your personal liability is generally limited to the amount of money you have invested in the company. Should the business fail or face a lawsuit, creditors can typically only go after the LLC's assets, not your personal property. This protection is the single most important reason to formalize your business.

Beyond liability protection, the LLC is celebrated for its flexibility. By default, an LLC's profits and losses are "passed through" to its owners (called "members"), who report them on their personal tax returns. This avoids the "double taxation" issue that can affect corporations. Furthermore, an LLC can elect to be taxed in different ways. You can choose to be taxed as a sole proprietorship (if you're a single member), a partnership (if you have multiple members), or even as an S-Corp or C-Corp, which offers strategic tax planning opportunities we'll discuss shortly.

LLCs are also relatively simple to set up and maintain compared to corporations. The filing requirements are less stringent, and the internal governance can be tailored to your specific needs. This makes the LLC an excellent choice for many bootstrapped startups, consulting businesses, or AI service companies that do not plan to seek venture capital funding in the immediate future.

The Tax-Savvy Option: The S Corporation (S-Corp)

The S Corporation is not a legal business structure in the same way an LLC is. Rather, it is a special tax election that can be made by either a C-Corporation or an LLC. When an LLC elects to be taxed as an S-Corp, it can offer a significant tax advantage for profitable businesses.

Here's how it works: In a standard LLC, all profits are passed through to the owners and are subject to self-employment taxes (Social Security and Medicare). In an S-Corp, you, as the owner-employee, must pay yourself a "reasonable salary" for the work you do. This salary is subject to regular employment taxes. However, any profits remaining in the company after all expenses (including your salary) are paid can be distributed to you as a "dividend." These dividends are not subject to self-employment taxes. For a business generating significant profit, this can result in thousands of dollars in tax savings.

This tax benefit comes with a strict set of rules. An S-Corp can have no more than 100 shareholders, all of whom must be U.S. citizens or resident aliens. It can also only have one class of stock. This last rule is a deal-breaker for most startups that plan to raise venture capital, as investors almost always require a different class of stock (preferred stock) with special rights. The S-Corp is therefore best suited for profitable, U.S.-based businesses that plan to remain closely held by a small group of founders.

The Venture Capital Standard: The C Corporation (C-Corp)

The C Corporation is the most complex of these structures, but it is the undisputed standard for any startup that intends to raise investment from venture capitalists (VCs) or angel investors. A C-Corp is a completely separate legal and taxable entity from its owners. It can sue, be sued, enter into contracts, and is taxed on its own profits.

The main reason investors insist on the C-Corp structure is its flexibility in ownership. C-Corps can issue different classes of stock. This allows founders to hold "common stock" while investors receive "preferred stock," which comes with special privileges like liquidation preferences (they get their money back first in a sale) and anti-dilution protection. This ability to create complex capital structures is essential for funding rounds. Ownership is also easily transferable through the sale of stock, and there are no restrictions on the number or type of shareholders, making it easy to accept investment from individuals, funds, and even other companies worldwide.

The primary drawback of a C-Corp is "double taxation." The corporation pays taxes on its profits at the corporate level. Then, if it distributes those profits to shareholders as dividends, the shareholders pay personal income tax on that money. However, for most high-growth AI startups, this is a theoretical problem. These companies typically reinvest all of their profits back into the business to fuel growth, so there are no dividends to tax. The long-term goal is not to pay dividends but to sell the company or go public, at which point the capital gains are taxed differently.

Business Entity Comparison

Feature	LLC	S-Corp	C-Corp
Personal Liability	Limited	Limited	Limited
Taxation	Pass-through (flexible election)	Pass-through (with salary/ dividend split)	Double taxation (corporate + shareholder)
Ease of Setup	Relatively Simple	Complex (requires tax election)	Complex (more formalities
Best for VCs?	No (must convert to C-Corp)	No (strict ownership rules)	Yes (standard for funding)

The Nuts and Bolts of Filing: Your Startup Checklist

Once you've chosen your entity type with the help of your legal and financial advisors, it's time to make it official. The process involves a series of steps that, while seemingly administrative, are crucial for establishing your company's legal standing and operational readiness.

First, you must choose a state for incorporation. You can file in the state where you live and operate, which is often the simplest choice for an LLC. However, for C-Corps planning to seek investment, the default choice is overwhelmingly Delaware. More than half of all U.S. publicly traded companies are incorporated in Delaware, not because they are located there, but because Delaware has a highly developed and predictable body of corporate law and a specialized court, known as the Court of Chancery, that deals exclusively with corporate disputes. This predictability is very attractive to investors.

Next, you will file your formation documents with the Secretary of State in your chosen state. For an LLC, this document is typically called the "Articles of Organization." For a C-Corp, it's the "Certificate of Incorporation." These documents are usually short and state the company's name, address, and registered agent (a person or service designated to receive official legal correspondence). You can file these yourself online, but services like Stripe Atlas, Clerky, or a qualified attorney can handle this process to ensure it's done correctly.

With your company officially formed, you need to get an Employer Identification Number (EIN) from the IRS. An EIN is like a Social Security Number for your business. It is absolutely essential for opening a business bank account, hiring employees, and filing your business tax returns. Getting an EIN is free and can be done in minutes through the IRS website. Do not pay a third-party service for this.

The moment your EIN is issued, your next stop should be the bank. You must open a dedicated business bank account. This is not an optional step. Commingling your personal and business funds, paying for business expenses from your personal account or vice-versa, is the fastest way to "pierce the corporate veil" and lose the liability protection you just worked to create. All business revenue must go into this account, and all business expenses must be paid from it.

Finally, you need to investigate local registrations and licenses. Depending on your city, county, and state, you may need to obtain a general business license to operate legally. If your business name is different from your official

LLC or corporate name (for example, your LLC is "XYZ Innovations, LLC" but you operate as "ClientFlow AI"), you will likely need to file a "Doing Business As" (DBA) or "Fictitious Name" registration.

Essential Legal Documents for an AI Business

Forming the entity is just the beginning. To govern your company and protect it from the unique risks associated with AI, you need a set of foundational legal documents. These are not generic templates to be copied and pasted from the internet. They should be drafted or at least reviewed by a lawyer to fit your specific business.

The Internal Rule book: Operating Agreement and Bylaws

For an LLC, the Operating Agreement is the single most important internal document. For a corporation, the equivalent is the Bylaws. These documents are the internal rule books that dictate how the company will be governed. Even if you are a single-founder company, you need one. It helps prove to courts that your business is a legitimate, separate entity.

For multi-founder companies, this document is non-negotiable. It should clearly define:

Ownership and Equity: The percentage of the company each founder owns.

Roles and Responsibilities: Who is responsible for what within the company.

Voting Rights: How major decisions will be made.

Profit and Loss Distribution: How profits will be divided among the owners.

Buy-Sell Provisions: What happens if a founder wants to leave, becomes disabled, or

passes away. This section pre-negotiates the terms for buying out a founder's shares, preventing incredibly difficult situations down the road.

Your Contract with the World: Terms of Service and Privacy Policy

When you launch your AI product, you are inviting the public to interact with a powerful and complex piece of technology. You must set the rules for that interaction. Your Terms of Service (ToS) also called Terms of Use, is the legal contract between your company and your users. For an AI business, this document is especially critical and must address several key issues.

It needs to define ownership of inputs and outputs. If a user uploads their data to your service (the input), who owns it? When your AI generates a result (the output), who owns that? Is it the user, your company, or is it in the public domain? There is no single answer; you must define your policy clearly. It also needs a robust Acceptable Use Policy that explicitly prohibits users from using your AI to create harmful, illegal, or unethical content, such as hate speech, misinformation, or non-consensual deepfakes.

Crucially, your ToS must include a Disclaimer of Warranty and Limitation of Liability. AI is not perfect. It can make mistakes, "hallucinate" facts, and produce flawed results. Your terms must state that you provide the service "as-is" and are not responsible for any damages that arise from a user's reliance on the AI's output. This clause is a vital piece of your legal shield.

Alongside your ToS, you must have a Privacy Policy. This is a legal requirement under laws like Europe's GDPR and the California Consumer Privacy Act (CCPA). This document must transparently explain to your users what personal data you collect, why you are collecting it, how you use it, how you protect it, and with whom you share it.

For an AI company, you need to be particularly clear about how you use data for training. If you plan to use customer inputs to further train and improve your AI models, you must disclose this and, in some jurisdictions, get explicit consent. The policy must also detail how users can exercise their data rights, such as the right to access or delete their information. Mishandling user data is one of the fastest ways for an AI startup to face massive fines and reputational ruin.

Protecting the Company: Founder Agreements

For businesses with more than one founder, a verbal agreement and a handshake are not enough. You need formal Founder Agreements that protect the company itself. The most important of these is a Restricted Stock Purchase Agreement which includes vesting provisions.

Vesting means that founders earn their equity over a period of time, rather than owning it all on day one. A typical vesting schedule is four years with a one-year "cliff." This means you get 0% of your stock if you leave within the first year. On your one-year anniversary (the cliff), 25% of your stock vests. The remaining 75% then vests in monthly or quarterly increments over the next three years. Vesting protects the company and the remaining founders if one co-founder decides to leave early. Without it, a founder could leave after two months and still own a huge chunk of a company they are no longer helping to build.

These agreements should also include an Intellectual Property (IP) Assignment clause. This clause legally transfers the ownership of any inventions, code, or work product created by the founders related to the business to the company. This ensures that the company, not the individual founders, owns the valuable AI technology it's built upon, which is essential for any future sale or investment.

* * *

9

Workflow Design: Integrating AI Agents

You have navigated the foundational stages of entrepreneurship and in doing so, an abstract idea has been sharpened into a specific, validated problem. You have explored the digital landscape and selected your AI tools. You've built a prototype, proving your concept is viable. You've even given your venture a name, a brand, and the legal armor of a formal business entity. Your business now exists on paper. The next step is to make it exist in practice. It's time to design the engine that will power its daily operations; the set of repeatable processes that transform your AI solution from a clever trick into a reliable, scalable service.

This is the art and science of workflow design. A workflow is the operational blueprint of your business. It is the choreographed sequence of tasks, decisions, and automations that deliver value to your customer consistently, every single time. Without a well-designed workflow, your business is just a collection of powerful tools with no instructions. With one, you can create a lean, efficient, and automated system where AI agents act as tireless digital employees, executing complex processes so you can focus on growing the business rather than just running it.

The journey from a successful prototype to a robust workflow is a critical

77

leap. A prototype, like the one we built in the case study, is a proof of concept. Its purpose is to answer the question, "Can this be done?" You might have manually uploaded the files, tweaked the AI prompts on the fly, and copy-pasted the output to create a single, impressive result. A workflow, on the other hand, is built to answer the question, "Can this be done a hundred times a day with minimal human intervention?" It demands a shift in thinking from one-off creation to systematic production.

This transition requires you to zoom out from the individual tools and look at the entire end-to-end process. You must anticipate every step, from the moment a customer signs up to the moment they receive their final deliverable. You need to account for variations, potential errors, and the necessary hand-offs between automated tasks and human oversight. Designing this system is not about you being a better user of a single AI tool; it's about you becoming an architect of an entire automated process. The AI agent is a powerful component, but it's the design of the assembly line it works on that creates real business value.

The Anatomy of an Automated Workflow

Before you can build your automated engine, you must first create a blueprint. The most effective way to do this is to visually map your process. This doesn't require complex software; a whiteboard, a large piece of paper, or a simple online diagramming tool will suffice. The act of drawing the workflow forces you to think through the logic and identify gaps you might otherwise miss. Every robust workflow, regardless of its purpose, can be broken down into four essential components: Triggers, Inputs, Actions, and Outputs.

The Trigger is the event that initiates the workflow. It's the starting pistol for the entire process. A trigger can be a customer action, like submitting a form on your website or making a purchase. It can be a time-based event, such as "every Monday at 9 a.m." It can also be an event in another software application, like a new file being added to a Google Drive folder or a new email arriving from a specific address. Defining a clear trigger is the first step in automation, as it tells your system precisely when to wake up and get to work.

Once triggered, the workflow needs raw materials to work with. These are the Inputs. Inputs are the data and documents required to complete the process. For our ClientFlow AI service, the inputs for an on-boarding workflow would be the new client's company name, their email address, and the specific service they purchased. For an AI that summarizes articles, the input would be the URL of the article. Clearly defining your inputs is crucial because they become the variables that your AI agents and automation tools will manipulate.

The core of the workflow is the sequence of Actions. These are the individual steps and decisions that transform the inputs into a valuable result. This is where you will integrate your AI agents. An action sequence could be as simple as "Take the input text and feed it to an AI to generate a summary." More realistically, it will be a multi-step process involving several tools. For example: 1) Extract text from an uploaded PDF. 2) Feed the text to AI Agent A to identify key themes. 3) Feed those key themes to AI Agent B to write a draft report. 4) Save the draft report in a specific folder. 5) Send a Slack notification to a human for review.

Finally, every workflow must produce a tangible Output. The output is the final, valuable result that is delivered to the customer or used internally. It's the finished report, the populated dashboard, the sent email, or the updated record in your CRM. The output is the culmination of the entire process and the tangible evidence of the value you provide. A well-defined output is measurable, allowing you to confirm that the workflow has successfully completed its job.

Mapping Your Core Business Processes

With this framework in mind, you can begin to map the essential workflows that will form the operational backbone of your business. Most service-based AI startups will rely on a few key types of workflows. By designing these systems from the outset, you build scalability into your company's DNA.

One of the most critical processes is Data Intake and Client On-boarding. This is the first impression a customer has of your service, and it's an area where automation can provide immense value. Instead of a series of manual emails, you can design a workflow that automates the entire experience. The trigger could be a successful payment via Stripe. The workflow would then automatically create a new customer record in your CRM, generate a branded portal (as we did with FuseBase), and send a welcome email containing a unique link to that portal. This ensures every single customer receives the same professional, organized welcome without any manual effort.

Inside the portal, the workflow continues. You can design it to automatically collect necessary files and information from the client. When the client uploads a document, it triggers a sub-workflow that renames the file according to a standard convention, files it in the correct folder, and updates a checklist to show the task as complete. This kind of systematic data intake not only saves you hours of administrative work but also dramatically reduces the chance of human error. It creates a smooth, predictable experience for your client and provides your AI agents with the structured data they need to do their job.

Another common workflow category is Automated Content and Report Generation. Many AI businesses are built on the promise of turning raw data into polished, insightful content. A workflow is what makes this promise deliverable at scale. Imagine a service that provides weekly social media analytics reports for small businesses. A time-based trigger would kick off the workflow every Friday afternoon. The workflow would automatically pull the latest data from the client's social media accounts via their APIs.

This raw data becomes the input for your AI agent. The agent, trained on your specific methodology for interpreting analytics, would then perform a series of actions: analyze the data for trends, identify the best-performing posts, and generate a narrative summary of the week's activity. The output wouldn't just be a spreadsheet; it would be a professionally formatted PDF report, complete with the client's logo, which is then automatically emailed to them. This transforms a high-effort consulting task into a fully automated, high-margin product.

Finally, every business needs a workflow for Customer Inquiries and Basic Support. As your business grows, you cannot personally answer every single question. This is a perfect job for a trained AI agent. The trigger is an incoming question, whether it arrives via a chat widget on your website, an email to your support address, or a comment inside a client portal. The input is the text of the customer's question.

The first action is to route the question to an AI agent that has been trained on a comprehensive knowledge base of your product, services, and policies. The agent attempts to answer the question directly. If it provides an answer, the workflow might follow up with a simple "Was this helpful?" to gather feedback. This is the first line of defense, handling the 80% of common, repetitive questions. If the agent cannot answer the question, however, the workflow doesn't just fail; it proceeds to the next action, which is to escalate the issue. It can automatically create a support ticket in a system like Zendesk or Trello, assigning it to a human and including the full context of the customer's question and the AI's failed attempt to answer.

AI Agents as Your Digital Workforce

The true power of modern workflow design comes from treating AI agents not as passive tools but as active, configurable members of your team. You are their manager. Your job is to define their roles, provide them with the resources they need to succeed, and integrate them into the broader team of software applications that run your business.

The first step in managing your digital workforce is Training and Resource Management. Just as you wouldn't ask a new employee to start working without any training, you cannot expect an AI agent to perform a task without a well-curated set of resources. This goes beyond the general "knowledge base" we've discussed. For a specific workflow, you must provide the agent with workflow-specific information. This might include templates for the reports it needs to generate, checklists for the steps it needs to follow, and examples of "what good looks like" for its outputs.

For instance, an AI agent tasked with drafting marketing emails needs more than just product information. It needs a "swipe file" of your best-performing past emails. It needs to be told about the target audience for this specific campaign. It needs to understand the desired tone and the specific call to action. By feeding the agent this context as part of the workflow's inputs, you are equipping it to perform its task with a much higher degree of accuracy and relevance. This training is not a one-time event; as you learn what works, you should continuously update the agent's resource library.

Next, you must clearly define the Agent's Role and Permissions. Not every digital employee should have the keys to the entire kingdom. A key concept in workflow design is the "human-in-the-loop" model. This means that you strategically place human review and approval points at critical junctures in the process. An AI agent might be given the role of "Draft Creator." It can analyze data, write a first draft of a report, and save it for review. However, it does not have the permission to send that report directly to the client.

The workflow is designed to pause after the agent completes its draft. It then sends a notification to you or a team member with a link to the draft. You can then quickly review the document, make any necessary edits, and click an "Approve" button. This approval is the trigger for the next stage of the workflow, which then proceeds to send the final document to the client. This approach gives you the best of both worlds: the massive time-saving benefit of AI-powered creation and the quality control and peace of mind of human oversight.

The final piece of the puzzle is connecting your AI agent to the outside world. An agent that can only "think" inside its own platform is of limited use. An agent that can Read and Write Data Across Your Entire Tech Stack is a superstar employee. This is accomplished through integrations. Modern no-code AI platforms have native integrations with hundreds of other applications. For everything else, there are "digital duct tape" services like Zapier or Make.

These services act as universal translators, allowing your different software tools to talk to each other. In a workflow, you can have your AI agent finish a task and then use Zapier to perform the next action: create a new row in a Google Sheet, update a customer record in your Airtable CRM, or post a message in a client's dedicated Slack channel. This ability to orchestrate actions across multiple platforms is what allows you to build truly end-to-end automations that mirror and replace complex manual business processes.

Designing for Failure: The Importance of Exception Handling

A common mistake in workflow design is creating a "happy path" diagram that assumes everything will work perfectly every time. In the real world, this is never the case. Files will be uploaded in the wrong format, data will be missing, and AIs will occasionally produce nonsensical output. A professional-grade workflow is not just designed to succeed; it is also designed to handle failure gracefully. This is known as exception handling.

For every automated step in your workflow, you must ask yourself, "What happens if this fails?" The answer should never be "nothing." Your workflow needs to have conditional logic and fallback paths built into it. For example, consider a workflow that uses an AI agent to extract data from an uploaded invoice. What happens if a client uploads a blurry, unreadable photo of the invoice? If the AI agent tries and fails to read the document, the workflow shouldn't just stop.

Instead, it should follow a pre-defined "error path." This path might include a series of actions: 1) Save the unreadable file to a special "Needs Manual Review" folder. 2) Update the status of the task in the client portal to "Action Required." 3) Send an automated, polite email to the client saying, "We're having trouble reading the invoice you uploaded. Could you please provide a clearer copy?" 4) Send a notification to an internal team member to let them know about the issue. This turns a potential failure and customer support headache into a managed, automated process.

This principle applies to the AI's output as well. You can build quality control checks directly into your workflow. For example, after an AI generates a summary, a subsequent action could be another AI call that asks a different, simpler model: "Does the following text contain any placeholders like '[INSERT DETAIL HERE]'?" If the check comes back positive, it indicates an incomplete generation. The workflow can then either attempt to run the generation again or, more safely, flag it for human review. Building these automated checks and balances creates a more resilient and reliable system.

A Concrete Example: The "AI Research Assistant" Workflow

To bring these concepts together, let's design a workflow for a fictional service called "Insight AI." This B2B service offers to create detailed research reports on any given topic for marketing agencies.

The Trigger for the workflow is a new entry in a "Research Requests" database in Airtable. The agency client fills out a simple form with the topic, the key questions they want answered, and the desired length of the report.

The Inputs are the topic, the list of questions, and the report length from the Airtable record.

Now, the Actions begin, orchestrated by a workflow tool like Make:

1. Acknowledge and Update: The workflow first updates the Airtable record's status to "In Progress." It then sends a confirmation email to the client: "We have received your research request for '[Topic]' and our AI assistant has begun its work."

2. AI-Powered Search: The workflow takes the topic and key questions and feeds them to a specialized AI agent connected to a web search API. The agent's instruction is: "Perform 10 web searches to find the most relevant and authoritative articles, studies, and statistics related to the following topic and questions. Return a list of the top 10 URLs."

3. Content Ingestion: The workflow takes the list of 10 URLs. It then runs a loop, visiting each URL and using a web scraping tool to extract the full text content from each page. This text is stored for the next step.

4. AI Summarization and Synthesis: The collected text from all 10 sources is fed as a large block of context to a powerful AI agent (like one from FuseBase or a similar platform). The agent's prompt is complex: "You are a world-class research analyst. Using ONLY the provided text, write a cohesive, well-structured report of [Report Length] words that answers the following [Key Questions]. Start with an executive summary. Use headings for each question. Cite your sources by referencing the original URL where the information was found. Do not invent any information."

5. Human-in-the-Loop Review: The AI-generated report is saved as a

Google Doc in a folder named "Drafts for Review." The workflow then posts a message in a private Slack channel: "New Insight AI report for '[Client Name]' on '[Topic]' is ready for review: [Link to Google Doc]."

6. Approval and Delivery: A human team member reviews the draft, fact-checks the key points against the sources, and makes any necessary edits for tone and clarity. Once satisfied, they change the status of the Airtable record to "Approved for Delivery."

7. Final Output: This status change is the trigger for the final part of the workflow. It takes the approved Google Doc, converts it to a professionally branded PDF using a template, and emails it to the client with a message: "Your Insight AI research report on '[Topic]' is complete. Please find it attached." The Airtable record is marked as "Delivered."

This entire process, which would take a human researcher many hours, is reduced to a 15-minute review. It's a scalable, repeatable, and high-value service built not just on a clever AI, but on a thoughtfully designed workflow. This is the operational core of a modern AI-based business. It's a system you design once and then deploy endlessly, allowing you to deliver exceptional value to your customers with unprecedented efficiency.

* * *

10

Testing, Feedback, and Continuous Improvement

You have now officially constructed your business. The legal documents are filed, the brand has a name and a face, and you've designed a sophisticated workflow that choreographs a sequence of automated tasks and AI-driven actions. On your whiteboard and within the dashboards of your chosen tools, this system looks perfect. It's a clean, logical, and efficient machine ready to deliver value. There is, however, one small problem: it has never encountered a real human being. All of your work up to this point, no matter how well-researched, is a collection of elegant hypotheses. Now it is time to expose those hypotheses to the messy, unpredictable, and ultimately truthful reality of the marketplace.

This chapter marks the transition from design to deployment. It's about taking your carefully constructed workflow off the drawing board and putting it into the hands of real people to see what happens. This is not a grand, public launch with fanfare and press releases. It is the exact opposite. It is a quiet, controlled, and intensely focused period of testing known as a pilot program or a closed beta. The goal is not to sell; the goal is to learn. You are inviting a small, hand-picked group of users behind the curtain to help you find the flaws, validate the value, and polish your service before you ask the wider world to pay for it.

The process of testing, feedback, and iteration is the engine of a modern startup. It is a continuous loop that transforms a good idea into a great business. In the past, companies would spend years building a product in secret, only to launch it and discover their core assumptions were wrong. Today, using no-code tools and AI agents, you can move from a workflow concept to a live pilot test in a matter of days. This agility allows you to learn faster, pivot smarter, and build a business that is resilient because it is forged in the crucible of real-world user feedback.

Your First Product: The Minimum Viable Service

Before you can test anything, you need something tangible to put in front of your pilot users. This is your Minimum Viable Product, or MVP. In the context of an AI-based service business, it's often more useful to think of this as a Minimum Viable Service (MVS). You are not necessarily building a self-contained piece of software; you are delivering a complete, end-to-end service experience that is powered by the workflow you designed in the previous chapter. The MVP, in this case, is the live, functioning version of that workflow, packaged up for your first clients.

The key word here is "Minimum." The goal is not to build every feature you've ever dreamed of. The goal is to deliver the core value proposition of your service in the simplest way possible. If your service promises to turn meeting notes into project plans, your MVP must do exactly that, and nothing more. Ancillary features like team management, advanced reporting, or multiple language support can wait. The central question your MVP must answer is: does this core function provide enough value that someone will use it and, eventually, pay for it?

For your initial pilot, your MVS might not even be fully automated. It's perfectly acceptable, and often strategically wise, to use the "Wizard of Oz" technique at this stage. Your client-facing portal might look slick and automated, but behind the scenes, you might still be manually triggering parts of the workflow, copy-pasting data between two tools that aren't yet integrated, or giving the AI's output a quick human review before it's sent to the client. This is not cheating; it is a lean and intelligent way to test the entire service experience before you invest the time in automating every last step. The customer experiences the full value, and you get to learn which parts of the workflow are most critical to automate first.

Assembling Your Pilot Crew

The success of your pilot program depends entirely on the quality of your testers. You are not looking for passive consumers; you are recruiting active collaborators. These are the people who will provide the raw material, the feedback, the criticism, the confusion, that you will use to refine your service. The ideal pilot user is a perfect match for the Ideal Customer Profile you developed in Chapter 5. They have the exact problem you are trying to solve, they understand the pain, and they are motivated to find a better way.

So where do you find these pioneers? Your first port of call should be the list of people you interviewed back in Chapter 1 when you were validating the problem. These individuals have already invested their time in helping you understand their world. They are primed and likely interested to see what you've built. Reconnect with them, remind them of your earlier conversation, and explain that you've created a potential solution and would be honored if they would be among the first to try it.

Your professional network on platforms like LinkedIn is another rich source. Look for contacts who fit your ICP and reach out with a personal message. Emphasize that you are not selling anything, but are looking for expert feedback from a select group before a public launch. People are often flattered to be asked for their expert opinion and are willing to help.

When you invite someone to your pilot program, you must be crystal clear about the "deal." This is a two-way street. In exchange for free or heavily discounted access to your service for a defined period (e.g., three months), they agree to provide you with detailed, honest feedback. Set the expectations upfront. Let them know that this is a beta version, that some things might not work perfectly, and that their primary role is to help you find and fix those imperfections. Frame them as co-creators on a mission to build the perfect tool for their industry. This framing encourages a sense of ownership and leads to much higher quality feedback. Aim for a small, manageable group for your first pilot, somewhere between five and ten clients is ideal. This is a large enough sample to see patterns, but small enough that you can maintain a personal, high-touch relationship with each one.

The Mechanisms of Feedback Collection

Once your pilot users are on-boarded and using your service, your most important job begins: listening. You must become a systematic and relentless collector of feedback. Simply asking "So, what do you think?" is not enough. You need to employ a mix of methods to gather both qualitative and quantitative data, painting a complete picture of the user experience.

Qualitative Insights: The "Why" Behind the Clicks

Qualitative feedback gives you the rich, narrative context that numbers alone can never provide. It helps you understand the user's motivations, frustrations, and the "why" behind their actions.

The single most valuable technique for gathering qualitative data is the live observational session. Schedule a 30-minute video call with a pilot user and ask them to share their screen as they use your service to complete a real task. Ask them to "think aloud," narrating their thoughts, expectations, and reactions as they go. Your role is not to guide them, but to shut up and watch. Where do they hesitate? What do they click on that you didn't expect? What question do they ask that reveals a flaw in your user interface? These sessions are an unvarnished window into how a real user experiences your product, and the insights they generate are pure gold.

Structured feedback interviews are another vital tool. Schedule regular, short check-in calls (perhaps every two weeks) with each pilot user. Prepare a short list of open-ended questions designed to elicit stories, not just "yes" or "no" answers.

"Can you walk me through the last time you used the service? What was the outcome?"

"Was there any point in the process where you felt stuck or unsure what to do next?"

"If you had a magic wand and could change one thing about the service, what would it
 be?"

"How did the AI's output compare to what you were expecting?"

Record these interviews (with permission) so you can go back and analyze the specific language users use to describe their problems and your solution. This language is what you will later use in your marketing copy.

Finally, use simple in-app feedback forms to capture immediate reactions. After a key action, like the delivery of an AI-generated report, you can include a simple, two-question survey. Question one can be a rating scale: "How satisfied were you with this report? (1-5)." Question two should be an open text box: "What would have made it better?" This captures feedback in the moment, while the experience is still fresh in the user's mind.

Quantitative Data: The "What" and "How Much"

While qualitative feedback provides the stories, quantitative data provides the hard evidence. It helps you move beyond anecdotes and measure your progress objectively. Even in an early pilot, you can track a few key metrics that serve as vital health indicators for your service.

Usage and Engagement is the most basic measure of value. Are people actually using your service? Track simple metrics like the number of times a pilot user logs in per week, the number of core tasks they complete (e.g., reports generated, workflows run), or the number of documents they upload. If a user isn't engaging with your service, it's a strong signal that it is not yet solving a painful enough problem.

Task Success Rate measures the effectiveness of your workflow. For the core task of your service, what percentage of the time does the user successfully complete it without needing help? If you have an AI agent designed to answer questions, what percentage of the time does it provide a correct answer versus escalating to a human? A low success rate is a clear indicator of friction in your workflow or a flaw in your AI's configuration.

Time savings is the holy grail metric for most B2B AI services. It is the most direct measure of your Return on Investment (ROI). To calculate this, you first need a baseline. During your on-boarding call with a pilot user, ask them, "How long does this process currently take you to do manually?" Then, after they have used your service for a few weeks, ask them how long it takes now. The difference is your value proposition in a single number. Being able to say, "Our pilot users saved an average of 4 hours per week," is an incredibly powerful statement.

Lastly, you can use established methodologies to measure overall satisfaction. The Net Promoter Score (NPS) is a simple but powerful tool. You ask one question: "On a scale of 0-10, how likely are you to recommend our service to a friend or colleague?" Users who give a score of 9 or 10 are "Promoters" as they have ranked the likelihood to be the highest, 7-8 are "Passives," and 0-6 are "Detractors." Your NPS is the percentage of Promoters minus the percentage of Detractors. It provides a single, high-level number that tracks overall sentiment over time.

The Iteration Cycle: Closing the Feedback Loop

Collecting feedback is pointless if you don't act on it. The final, crucial step is to build a system for turning those insights into tangible improvements. This is the iteration engine that drives your business forward. It's a continuous cycle of listening, analyzing, prioritizing, and implementing.

First, you need a central place to organize all incoming feedback. This doesn't need to be a complex system. A simple Trello board or an Airtable database will work perfectly. Create a new card or record for every single piece of feedback you receive, whether it comes from an interview, a survey, or an observation session. Capture the user's verbatim quote and note who gave the feedback and when.

Next, you must triage and categorize this raw feedback. Not all feedback is created equal. You can use a simple tagging system to sort it into a few key buckets:

Bug: Something is broken and not working as intended. The AI is crashing, a button
doesn't work, a file won't upload. These are typically the highest priority.

Usability Issue: The feature works, but it's confusing or difficult to use. A user didn't
know where to click, the instructions were unclear, the layout was illogical. These are
also high priority, as they create friction that can cause users to abandon your service.

Feature Request: A suggestion for a new capability that your service doesn't currently
have. These are valuable, but they need to be evaluated against your product roadmap.

Training Gap: The AI agent consistently fails to answer a specific type of

question or
makes a recurring mistake in its output. This signals a gap in its training data or its core
instructions.

Once your feedback is categorized, you can prioritize what to work on. You cannot act on everything at once. Focus your energy where it will have the greatest impact. A good framework is to prioritize tasks that will reduce the most user friction or deliver the most value. Fixing a critical bug that is blocking all of your pilot users is more important than adding a minor new feature that one person requested.

This is where the principle of "dropping low-ROI tools and doubling down on winners" comes into play. Your pilot test might reveal that a specific AI tool you chose for your workflow is consistently under-performing. Perhaps its transcription accuracy is too low, or its image generation is not realistic enough. The feedback gives you the data you need to make a tough decision: it's time to iterate on your own tech stack. You can then run a small experiment (as discussed in Chapter 3) to test a new tool for that specific job and, if it performs better, swap it into your main workflow.

Conversely, you might find that one particular feature is a huge hit. Perhaps your AI-generated executive summaries are so good that clients are copy-pasting them directly into their own board presentations. This is a signal to "double down." How can you make that feature even better? Can you offer different summary lengths? Can you allow users to specify the tone? This feedback helps you identify your "killer feature" and invest your resources accordingly.

Finally, and most importantly, you must close the loop with your pilot users. When you release a fix or an improvement based on someone's feedback, send them a personal email. "Hi Jane, remember how you mentioned it was confusing to find the 'Export to PDF' button? Based on your feedback, we've moved it to the top right of the screen. Let me know what you think!" This simple action has a profound effect. It shows your users that you are listening, that their feedback matters, and that they are having a real impact on the product. It turns them from mere testers into loyal, engaged advocates for your brand.

Graduating from the Pilot

A pilot program is not a permanent state. It is a temporary phase with a clear goal: to get your service ready for a public launch. So how do you know when you've reached that point? You need to define your "graduation criteria" before you even begin. These are the success signals that tell you it's time to move to the next level.

Your graduation checklist might include things like:

- **The task success rate for the core workflow is consistently above 95%.**
- **All major bugs and critical usability issues identified during the pilot have been resolved.**
- **Your NPS score has moved into positive territory, with more Promoters than Detractors.**
- **You have a clear, data-backed understanding of the ROI your service provides (e.g., "we save users X hours per month").**
- **You have at least three to five pilot users who have explicitly stated they would be willing to pay for the service when the free trial ends. This is the ultimate validation.**
- **You have collected a handful of powerful testimonials that you can use as social proof on your future landing page.**

Once you can confidently check these boxes, you have successfully navigated one of the most critical phases of building your business. You have replaced assumptions with evidence. You have transformed a brittle prototype into a robust service that has been tested under real-world conditions. Your business is no longer just an idea; it's a proven solution with a group of happy early customers who are ready to become your first paying clients.

* * *

11

Crafting Your Go-to-Market Strategy

The pilot program is over. The curtain has fallen on the private, controlled environment of beta testing, and your fledgling business is about to step onto the main stage. The feedback from your small, hand-picked group of users has been invaluable, allowing you to sand down the rough edges, fix the most glaring flaws, and confirm that your AI-powered service genuinely solves the problem you set out to address. You have turned your hypotheses into a functional, validated service. Now, you face an entirely new and exhilarating challenge: convincing complete strangers to use and, more importantly, pay for it.

This is the purpose of a Go-to-Market (GTM) strategy. It is your deliberate, coordinated plan for engaging the wider market and acquiring your first real, paying customers. It is the bridge between the sheltered world of product development and the chaotic reality of the marketplace. This is not the time for a "build it and they will come" mentality. Hope is not a strategy. A GTM plan is a series of calculated actions designed to introduce your solution to the specific audience you identified in Chapter 5, using the channels where they are most likely to be found, and speaking to them in a language that resonates with their needs.

Your approach will be a direct consequence of the business model you chose back in Chapter 6. The tactics used to attract a hundred small businesses to a B2B service are fundamentally different from those used to attract ten thousand individual users to a B2C app. There is no one-size-fits-all playbook. Your GTM strategy must be tailored to your unique business, your specific customer, and the value you have promised to deliver. This chapter will provide you with the tactical building blocks to construct that plan, turning your validated service into a commercially viable business.

Building Your Digital Storefront

Before you can invite guests to your party, you need a place for the party to happen. In the digital world, your primary venue is your landing page. This is more than just an online brochure; it is your 24/7 salesperson, your primary conversion tool, and the anchor for all your marketing efforts. All roads, whether from an ad, a social media post, or a direct email, will lead here. Before you launch any active campaigns, you must ensure this destination is ready to convert visitors into customers.

Your landing page must achieve several critical objectives in a matter of seconds. First, it must articulate your Value Proposition with absolute clarity. A new visitor should understand what you do and what's in it for them within five seconds of arrival. For this, you can utilize the "Jobs to Be Done" framework from Chapter 5. Don't lead with technical features; lead with the outcome. A headline like "AI-Powered Workflow Automation" is vague. A headline like "Stop Wasting Hours on Meeting Notes. Get AI-Generated Action Items Sent to Your Team Automatically!" is a value proposition. It speaks directly to a pain point and promises a specific, desirable result.

Next, your landing page must build immediate trust. This is where the work you did in your pilot program pays off. Social Proof is the most powerful trust signal you have. Scatter quotes and testimonials from your happy pilot users throughout the page. A simple, authentic quote like, "ClientFlow AI saved our team at least 5 hours in the first week. It's the most organized we've ever been with a new client" is infinitely more persuasive than any marketing copy you could write yourself. If you are a B2B business, ask one of your best pilot customers if you can develop their story into a more detailed Case Study. A dedicated page that outlines the client's problem, your solution, and the measurable results (e.g., "Innovate Corp reduced on-boarding paperwork errors by 90%") is a powerful asset you can link to from your main page.

Finally, your landing page needs a single, prominent Call to Action (CTA). Do not confuse visitors with multiple choices. Decide on the one action you want them to take and make the button for it unmissable. Whether it's "Start Your Free Trial," "Request a Demo," or "Sign Up Now," the CTA should be clear, compelling, and consistent. This digital storefront is your foundational marketing asset. It must be in place before you spend a single dollar or a single hour driving traffic to it.

The B2B Playbook: A Game of Spears, Not Nets

If you have chosen a Business-to-Business (B2B) or Business-to-Business-to-Consumer (B2B2C) model, your GTM strategy is not about shouting to the masses. It is about whispering to the right people. You are not casting a wide net, hoping to catch a few fish. You are carefully crafting a spear to target a specific, high-value catch. This requires a focused, often manual, and highly personalized approach. Your goal is not to get thousands of signups, but to start a handful of meaningful conversations with companies that perfectly match your Ideal Customer Profile.

The Art of Direct Outreach

For a B2B startup, your first ten, and likely your first fifty, customers will not come from a clever ad campaign. They will come from direct, thoughtful outreach. This is the grunt work of company building, and it is non-negotiable. Start by building a target list of one hundred companies that are a perfect fit for your ICP. Use tools like LinkedIn Sales Navigator, industry directories, or even manual Google searches to find companies of the right size, in the right industry, and in the right location.

Once you have your list of companies, you need to find the right person to contact within each one, your buyer persona. Your goal is to write a short, personalized email or LinkedIn message that demonstrates you've done your homework. Do not send a generic, copy-pasted blast. That is spam, and it will be ignored. Your message should have three parts.

First, the Personalized Hook. Spend two minutes researching the person or their company. Did they recently get promoted? Did their company just announce a new product? Did they write an interesting article on LinkedIn? Start your message by referencing this. "Hi Sarah, I saw your recent post on the challenges of scaling an agency team and it really resonated...". This immediately shows you are not a robot.

Second, the Problem Statement. Briefly connect their world to the problem you solve. "...Many agency leaders I speak with find that as they grow, client on-boarding becomes a major time sink. Manual follow-ups and scattered files start to get in the way of doing the actual creative work." This shows empathy and understanding of their pain.

Third, the Soft Call to Action. You are not asking for a sale. You are asking for a conversation. "I've been working on a new way to automate this process and would love to get your expert opinion on it for 15 minutes next week. Even if it's not a fit, you might find the approach interesting." By asking for their opinion rather than their money, you lower the barrier and appeal to their expertise. Track your outreach in a simple spreadsheet. Your goal is a conversation, not an immediate conversion.

Content Marketing: Your Trust-Building Engine

While direct outreach is your primary tool for short-term sales, content marketing is your engine for long-term growth and authority. The goal of content marketing in a B2B context is to educate your target customer and establish your company as the go-to expert in your specific niche. When a potential customer has a problem, you want your company's name to be the first one that comes to mind.

You don't need a massive content budget to do this effectively. Start by writing insightful articles that address the specific challenges and questions of your ICP. If you are selling ClientFlow AI, you should be writing articles with titles like "The Five Hidden Costs of a Messy Client On-boarding Process" or "A Step-by-Step Guide to Creating a Client Welcome Packet That Wows." The key is to provide genuine value, not a thinly veiled sales pitch. Answer the questions your customers are already typing into Google.

Post these articles on your company blog and share them on LinkedIn, where your target audience is most likely to be active. Engage in the comments. Use these articles as "air cover" for your direct outreach. You can include a link to a relevant article in your follow-up emails, providing additional value and demonstrating your expertise. Over time, this library of helpful content will become a magnet, drawing inbound leads to your business and making your sales conversations much warmer.

The B2C Playbook: Riding the Wave of Volume

If you are a Business-to-Consumer (B2C) company, your strategy is the inverse of B2B. A high-touch, personalized approach is not scalable. Your success depends on reaching a large volume of potential users efficiently and converting them with a friction-less experience. You are not hunting with a spear; you are looking for a current you can ride.

Winning the Search Game

For many B2C products, the journey begins with a problem typed into a search engine. Your job is to be the top answer. Search Engine Optimization (SEO) is the long-term strategy of creating content and structuring your website so that it ranks highly on search engines like Google for the keywords your customers use. Go back to the keyword research you did in Chapter 1. The phrases people use to describe their problems, "healthy meal planner app," "how to make a vacation itinerary," "bedtime stories for kids", are your targets.

Create high-quality blog posts, guides, or even simple free tools that are optimized for these keywords. For example, a company with an AI vacation planning app could write articles like "The Ultimate Guide to Planning a Two-Week Trip to Italy" or "10 Common Travel Planning Mistakes and How to Avoid Them." This content attracts users who are actively looking for a solution, making them highly qualified leads for your product. While SEO takes time to show results, it is one of the most sustainable and cost-effective ways to acquire B2C users.

Community, Virality, and Social Proof

B2C purchases are heavily influenced by trust and social validation. People want to use what other people are using. Your GTM strategy must be designed to generate and showcase this social proof.

First, identify the online "watering holes" where your target audience congregates. These could be subreddits, Facebook groups, or niche forums. Become an active and helpful member of these communities. Answer questions, participate in discussions, and build a reputation as a knowledgeable contributor. Only mention your product when it is a direct and helpful answer to someone's question. A recommendation from a trusted community member is far more powerful than an advertisement.

Second, encourage and amplify the voices of your early users. Make it incredibly easy for them to leave reviews or ratings. Display these testimonials and star ratings prominently on your landing page and app store listing. Run a referral program where existing users get a benefit (like a free month of service) for inviting their friends. This can create a "viral loop" where your own users become your most effective marketing channel.

For a significant launch push, consider a campaign on a product discovery site like Product Hunt. A successful launch on that platform can drive tens of thousands of curious early adopters to your site in a single day, providing a massive initial boost in traffic and visibility.

Partnerships and Paid Channels

To supplement your organic efforts, you can use paid channels to reach a wider audience. Influencer marketing can be particularly effective for B2C products. Find content creators on platforms like Instagram, TikTok, or YouTube whose audience perfectly matches your B2C persona. A single authentic video or post from a trusted influencer can drive more sign-ups than weeks of traditional advertising.

More traditional paid advertising on social media platforms can also be effective, provided you are disciplined. Use the detailed persona you created in Chapter 5 to build a highly targeted ad audience. Test different ad creatives and copy relentlessly to see what resonates. Start with a small budget. The goal of early advertising is not massive scale; it is learning. You are paying for data on which messages and images are most effective at converting your target audience.

AI as Your Marketing and Sales Force Multiplier

Regardless of your business model, you are building an AI-based business. It would be a missed opportunity not to use the power of AI to supercharge your own go-to-market efforts. Modern AI tools can act as a co-pilot for your marketing and sales activities, dramatically increasing your speed, efficiency, and effectiveness.

Think of AI as your tireless marketing intern. Need to write five different versions of an ad for a Facebook campaign? An AI text generator like Jasper or Copy.ai can produce them in seconds. Need a compelling image for a social media post? An AI image generator like Midjourney can create a dozen unique options in minutes. This is helpful for those who aren't as in tune with social media trends as you can directly instruct AI to give you inspiration for images that align with current trends to further focus and push your ad to success without the need for an entire marketing team. This allows you to test more ideas, faster, than you ever could on your own.

For your content marketing efforts, AI can be an invaluable research assistant and drafting partner. You can use an AI tool to analyze top-ranking articles on a given topic and generate a detailed outline for your own, more comprehensive piece. It can help you overcome writer's block by drafting initial paragraphs or suggesting different ways to phrase a complex idea. You, the human expert, still guide the process and provide the final polish and unique insights, but the AI handles 80% of the heavy lifting.

In the B2B sales process, AI can bring a new level of personalization to your outreach. There are tools that can analyze a prospect's LinkedIn profile and recent activity and suggest a highly personalized opening line for your email. This can be the difference between a message that gets a reply and one that gets instantly deleted.

You can also use the same kind of AI agent technology that powers your core service to build internal tools. Create an AI agent trained on all your marketing materials and case studies. Before a sales call, you can ask it, "What are the three best talking points for a conversation with a marketing agency of 20 people?" It can instantly synthesize the most relevant information, acting as your personal sales coach.

Your GTM strategy is your company's introduction to the world. It is the culmination of all the research, building, and testing you have done so far. By choosing the right tactics for your business model, building your foundational assets, and leveraging the power of AI to accelerate your efforts, you can move from the controlled environment of a pilot program to a sustainable, customer-generating business. It is a methodical process of outreach, content creation, and community building that, over time, will transform your initial ripple of activity into a wave of market adoption.

* * *

12

Pricing for Value and Scale

Of all the decisions you will make as a founder, none is more charged with emotion, fear, and consequence than setting your price. It is the single point where your confidence in your product, your understanding of your customer, and your business ambitions are distilled into a single number. It is the most direct and unfiltered communication of value you will ever make. Get it wrong, and you can cripple your business before it even has a chance to run. Get it right, and you create a powerful engine for sustainable growth.

Many founders, especially those from technical backgrounds, are deeply uncomfortable with this conversation. They see pricing as a grubby commercial necessity, a distraction from the elegant work of building the product itself. They fall into one of two traps: they either price based on a timid, cost-focused calculation, leaving vast sums of money on the table, or they pluck a number from thin air, hoping it sticks. Both approaches are paths to mediocrity.

This chapter is your guide to moving from fear and guesswork to a confident, strategic approach to pricing. We will dismantle the common myths and replace them with a practical framework for discovering, communicating, and capturing the value your AI service provides. This is not a dark art; it is a discipline that sits at the intersection of psychology, economics, and a deep understanding of the customer you serve. You've already done the hard work of identifying their problems and building a solution. Now, let's determine what that solution is truly worth.

The Most Common Mistake: The Folly of Cost-Plus Pricing

Before we explore how to price your service correctly, we must first quarantine the most common and destructive approach: cost-plus pricing. This is the method where you calculate your business costs, add a desired profit margin, and call that your price. An accountant might calculate that your server fees, software licenses, and API calls from third-party AI models cost you, on average, $10 per customer per month. A desire for a healthy 100% margin leads to a price of $20 per month. It seems logical, safe, and defensible. It is also completely wrong.

Cost-plus pricing is a relic of an industrial economy where the cost of raw materials and labor was the primary driver of price. In a digital, AI-driven business, your direct costs are often infinitesimally small compared to the value you create. Anchoring your price to your costs is like a brain surgeon basing their fee on the cost of the scalpel and anesthetic. The value is not in the tools used; it is in the outcome delivered.

Imagine your AI service automates a tedious reporting task for a financial analyst. Your direct API costs for generating one report might be fifty cents. The analyst, who earns $100 per hour, used to spend four hours creating this report manually. Your service saves them $400 worth of their time, frees them up for higher-value strategic work, and eliminates the risk of costly human errors in their spreadsheets. If you price your service at one dollar per report based on your costs, you are not just under-pricing; you are fundamentally misunderstanding the nature of your own business. You are selling a cheap commodity, not a high-value solution. This approach creates a race to the bottom, where you are forever trapped by your own expenses and unable to invest in growth, innovation, or providing exceptional support.

The Foundation of Modern Pricing: Selling the Outcome

The alternative, and the undisputed gold standard for any software or AI business, is value-based pricing. The core principle is simple: your price should be a fraction of the value you deliver to your customer. You are not selling API calls, processing cycles, or lines of code. You are selling a result. You are selling time back into your customer's day. You are selling increased revenue. You are selling reduced risk. You are selling peace of mind. Your price, therefore, should be anchored to the magnitude of that result.

This is why the work you did in the preceding chapters is so critical. You cannot determine a value-based price without a crystal-clear understanding of your Ideal Customer Profile (Chapter 5) and the "Job to Be Done" (Chapter 5) that they are hiring your product for. The value of saving one hour is different for a freelance graphic designer than it is for a partner at a major law firm. The value of acquiring one new lead is different for a local coffee shop than it is for an enterprise software company.

Quantifying this value is the first step. You need to build a "value case" for your product, starting with the most tangible metrics. This is your Hard ROI (Return on Investment).

Time Saved: This is often the easiest to calculate and the most powerful to communicate for B2B services. The formula is straightforward: (Hours saved per week/month) x (The effective hourly rate of the employee). During your pilot program (Chapter 10), this is a metric you should have been obsessively tracking. Being able to state, "Our pilot users saved an average of 10 hours per month," is the foundation of your value case.

Money Made: This can be measured in increased revenue from new leads, higher customer conversion rates, or the ability to handle more clients. If your AI helps an e-commerce store increase its conversion rate by just 1%, the monetary value can be enormous. This is harder to prove definitively at first, but it is a powerful metric to track through case studies.

Money Saved: This can be a reduction in spending on other software, a decreased need to hire additional staff, or the elimination of fines or fees due to compliance errors. If your AI service replaces three other subscription tools that cost a company a combined $300 per month, there is a clear and immediate value proposition.

Beyond these hard numbers lies the Soft ROI. This is the value that is harder to fit into a spreadsheet but is often just as important in the buying decision. This includes things like reduced stress for the user, increased professionalism in front of their clients, improved team morale because tedious work is automated, or the security of knowing a process is being handled consistently and correctly every time. While you can't put a direct dollar figure on these, you should use the language of these benefits in your marketing to appeal to the emotional side of the purchase.

A common rule of thumb in the software industry is the 10x Rule. Customers should perceive the value they receive to be at least ten times the price they pay. This gives them an overwhelming sense of getting a great deal and makes the purchase decision easy. So, if you can confidently demonstrate that your service provides $1,000 per month in quantifiable value (time saved, etc.), you can feel confident charging $100 per month. The customer gets a 10-to-1 return on their investment, and you have a sustainable, profitable business.

Choosing Your Pricing Structure: The Shape of Your Offer

Once you have a firm grasp of the value you provide, you must decide on the structure of your pricing model. This is about how you charge, which is a separate decision from how much you charge. The structure you choose will define how your revenue grows as your customers get more value from your service.

Flat-Rate Subscription: This is the simplest model. You offer one product at one price for everyone. For example, "$50 per month for everything." Its beauty is its simplicity. There is no confusion, and the sales process is straightforward. This model works best for products with a very clear, single use case and a relatively homogenous customer base. The primary risk is that you are leaving money on the table. A small business might find the price too high, while a large enterprise using the service heavily is getting an incredible bargain at your expense.

Tiered Pricing: This is the most common pricing model for software and AI businesses for a reason. You create two to four distinct plans (e.g., Basic, Pro, Enterprise), each with a different set of features and a different price point. This allows you to segment your market effectively. A small user can start on a cheaper plan, while a power user who needs more advanced features can upgrade to a more expensive one. This model provides a clear upgrade path for your customers as their needs grow, which means their value to your business also grows. The key to successful tiered pricing is choosing the right "value metric" to differentiate the tiers.

Usage-Based or Metered Pricing: In this model, customers pay directly for what they consume. This is the "pay-as-you-go" approach. The price is tied to a specific unit of consumption, such as the number of API calls made, the number of reports generated, the hours of audio transcribed, or the gigabytes of data processed. This model perfectly aligns your price with the value received. Customers love it because it feels fair, and it dramatically lowers the barrier to getting started. The major downside is unpredictability, both for your revenue forecasting and for your customer's budgeting. A customer who has a huge spike in usage one month can be hit with a surprisingly large bill, which can lead to churn.

Per-User Pricing: This is the classic B2B software model where you charge a monthly fee for each user or "seat" on an account. A team of five pays five times more than a solo user. This model is simple to understand and aligns well with value in collaborative tools, as more users often mean more value is being derived. The main drawback is that it can create friction and discourage adoption within a company. A manager might hesitate to invite more team members because it will increase the bill, which can limit the "stickiness" of your product within the organization.

The Most Important Pricing Decision: Your Value Metric

If you choose a tiered or usage-based model, the single most important decision you will make is selecting your value metric. This is the unit you are charging for. It is the axis upon which your entire pricing strategy pivots. A great value metric has three key characteristics: it aligns with the value the customer receives, it is easy for them to understand, and it grows as their usage and success with your product grows.

Choosing the wrong value metric can be disastrous. For example, charging based on the number of projects a user creates might seem logical for a project management tool. But if users start creating fewer, larger projects to avoid hitting a limit, your metric is actively discouraging them from using the product more deeply. Charging based on data storage can also be problematic if the storage itself is not the core value.

Let's consider some examples of strong value metrics for AI businesses:

For our ClientFlow AI service, a poor value metric would be the number of users. A good value metric would be the number of active client portals or the number of clients on-boarded per month. This ties the price directly to the core job the customer is hiring the service for.

For an AI-powered social media tool a weak value metric would be the number of posts drafted. A strong value metric would be the number of connected social media accounts. As an agency grows and manages more client accounts, its bill grows in line with the value it's receiving.

For an AI meeting summarizer the value metric is straightforward: the number of meetings transcribed or the number of transcription hours. It's a direct measure of consumption and value.

Spend a significant amount of time debating your value metric. It is the engine of your pricing model. Get it right, and your revenue will grow naturally alongside your most successful customers. Get it wrong, and you will create constant friction and be forced into painful pricing changes down the road.

The Finishing Touches: The Psychology of Pricing

Once you have determined your pricing strategy and structure, you must present it in a way that encourages a purchase. How your prices are displayed on your landing page can have a significant impact on your conversion rates. This is where you can leverage some well-understood principles of pricing psychology.

The Power of Three: Presenting three pricing tiers is a classic and effective strategy. It leverages a psychological bias known as "extremeness aversion," where people tend to avoid the cheapest and most expensive options and gravitate toward the middle. You can amplify this by labeling your middle tier as "Most Popular" or "Best Value," using social proof to guide the customer's decision.

The Decoy Effect: You can intentionally design one of your tiers to be a "decoy." For example, if your Pro plan is $99 and your Basic plan is $49, you might create a middle tier at $89 that is only marginally better than the Basic plan. Its purpose is not to be chosen; its purpose is to make the Pro plan at $99 look like an obviously superior deal in comparison.

The Magic of Annual Discounts: Always offer an annual subscription option at a significant discount to the monthly price (a 15-20% discount, framed as "get two months free," is standard). This has two huge benefits for you. First, it dramatically improves your cash flow by getting a full year's payment upfront. Second, it locks the customer in for a year, massively reducing churn and increasing their lifetime value (LTV). Make the annual toggle prominent on your pricing page.

Price Anchoring and the "Contact Us" Tier: For B2B businesses, it is common to have a high-end "Enterprise" tier with no public price, only a "Contact Us" button. This serves two purposes. First, it prevents sticker shock and allows you to craft a custom quote for high-value clients. Second, it acts as a price anchor. The mere existence of a very expensive enterprise option makes your self-serve tiers seem much more reasonable by comparison.

Charm Pricing: The practice of ending prices with the number nine (e.g., $49 instead of $50) is known as charm pricing. The theory is that customers perceive "$40-something" as significantly cheaper than "$50." While its effectiveness can be debated, especially in high-trust B2B sales, it is a prevalent and easy-to-test tactic, particularly for B2C products.

Your Pricing Page: Bringing It All Together

Let's design a hypothetical pricing page for "Insight AI," the research assistant service from Chapter 9, to illustrate these principles in action.

The page would have a clear headline: "Get Expert Research Reports, Instantly. Choose Your Plan." Below this, a toggle for "Monthly" and "Annual (Save 17%)" would be prominently displayed.

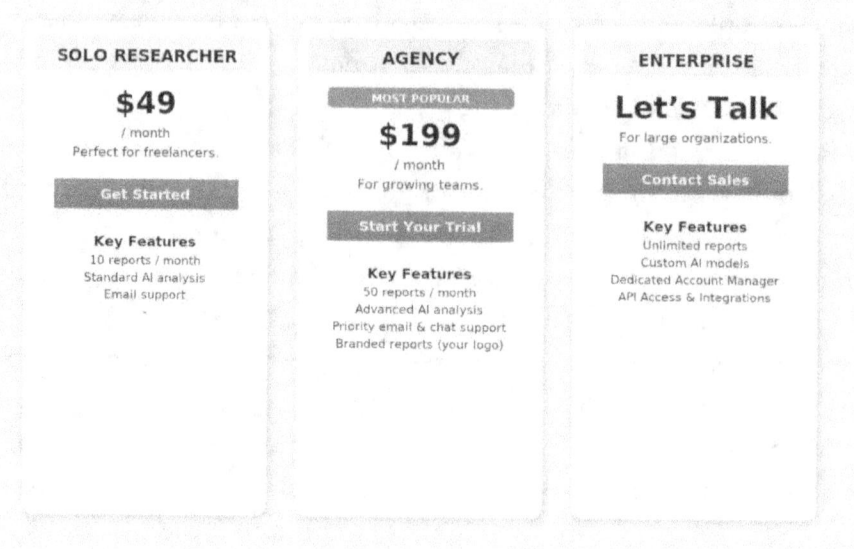

This pricing page uses tiered pricing, a clear value metric (number of reports), price anchoring (the Enterprise tier), social proof ("Most Popular"), and a clear call to action for each column. It's a strategic tool designed to convert visitors by clearly communicating value at different levels.

Pricing as a Continuous Journey

Your first pricing page is not a stone tablet. It is your best-educated guess, an initial hypothesis that must be tested in the real market. Pricing is not a one-time decision; it is an ongoing process of discovery and refinement. As you begin your go-to-market activities and have sales conversations, use them as opportunities for pricing research. Be direct. Ask your prospects, "Does this pricing seem fair for the value you'd be getting?" Their honest reaction, a quick nod, a hesitant pause, a sharp intake of breath, is priceless data.

As your product evolves and adds new capabilities, the value you provide increases. Therefore, your pricing should evolve as well. Plan to review and potentially adjust your pricing at least once a year. When you do raise prices for new customers, it is a gesture of goodwill to "grandfather" your earliest customers in at their original price. This rewards them for their loyalty and turns them into your most ardent supporters. By treating pricing as a dynamic, strategic function rather than a one-time task, you ensure that your business model remains healthy, profitable, and perfectly aligned with the ever-increasing value you bring to your customers.

* * *

13

Building Minimum Viable Products with AI

You have a plan. You have a brand. You have a price. You have a workflow diagram that looks like a masterpiece of logic and efficiency. On paper, your business is a well-oiled machine. The problem is, no business truly exists on paper. A business only becomes real when it delivers value to a customer, and that customer acknowledges the value in return. The time for theory is over. You must now build the first, functional, living version of your service, the version you will use to acquire your first real users and, ultimately, your first paying customers. This initial offering is your Minimum Viable Product, or MVP.

The concept of the MVP is one of the most powerful ideas in modern entrepreneurship, but it is also one of the most misunderstood. It is not simply a buggier, uglier version of your final product. An MVP is a strategic tool designed for one purpose: to achieve the maximum amount of validated learning about your customers with the minimum amount of effort. For an AI-based business, this concept takes on a new and exciting dimension. You don't need to spend six months and fifty thousand dollars on a team of developers to build your MVP. You can often assemble it in a week using the same no-code and AI tools you've already been experimenting with.

This is a crucial distinction. In this chapter, we are moving beyond the prototype we built in the case study. A prototype's job is to answer the internal question, "Is this technically possible?" An MVP's job is to answer the external question, "Is this valuable enough that someone will use it to solve their real-world problem?" This means the MVP must be robust enough to work, complete enough to deliver on your core promise, and simple enough to build quickly. It is the bridge from your internal workshop to the external marketplace.

The Two Flavors of Manual MVP: Concierge and Wizard of Oz

For an AI-powered service, your first MVP will almost certainly involve a significant amount of manual work from you, the founder. This is not a sign of failure; it is a sign of intelligence. By placing yourself directly in the middle of the workflow, you gain insights that are impossible to get from a distance. There are two primary strategies for building this human-powered first version: the Concierge MVP and the Wizard of Oz MVP.

The Wizard of Oz approach, which we touched on during the experimentation phase, involves creating a polished front-end interface that gives the illusion of full automation, while you are manually doing all the work behind the scenes. A customer fills out a form on a slick website, and a few minutes later, they receive a perfectly formatted AI-generated report via email. They believe a sophisticated machine did the work. In reality, you, the "wizard," were frantically copy-pasting their inputs into various AI tools and assembling the output yourself. This method is excellent for testing a specific user experience and gauging market demand for a seemingly automated solution.

The Concierge MVP is even more hands-on, and it makes no attempt to hide the human involvement. In fact, it embraces it. With this approach, you are not selling a product; you are delivering a white-glove, high-touch manual service. There is no automated front-end. Your first client might onboard via a phone call or a shared Google Doc. You personally walk them through the entire process, using your AI tools as your own personal superpowers to deliver the result. You become a one-person consulting agency, solving the client's problem manually to learn every single nuance of their needs and their desired outcome.

Let's illustrate with an example. Imagine your business, "LegalBrief AI," aims to help lawyers by taking a long legal document and creating a concise, two-page summary of the key arguments and precedents.

A Wizard of Oz MVP would involve a website with a secure upload portal. The lawyer uploads their document, the site shows a "processing" animation, and you manually run the document through your AI summarization prompt, clean up the output, and email the brief back to the lawyer. You are testing the demand for a self-serve tool.

A Concierge MVP would involve you telling your first lawyer client, "Email me your document. I will personally review it and send you back a two-page summary within 24 hours." You then use your AI tools to do the work, but the entire interaction is manual and conversational. You are testing the core value proposition and learning the exact requirements of a legal professional.

For most AI service businesses, the Concierge approach is the superior starting point. It forces you into direct, unfiltered contact with your customer's problem. You learn their vocabulary, their anxieties, and their definition of "good." You discover edge cases and complexities you could never have anticipated. These deep insights are the bedrock upon which you will later build your automated systems. You first become the expert human, and only then do you teach the machine to replicate your expertise.

The Three Layers of Your AI MVP

Whether you choose a Concierge or a Wizard of Oz approach, your MVP will consist of three fundamental layers. Your initial task is to assemble the simplest possible version of each layer, using off-the-shelf tools to get up and running as quickly as possible.

Layer 1: The "Front Door" (User Input & Interface)

This is how your customer initiates a request and provides you with the necessary information. The goal here is not to build a custom application; it is to create the lowest-friction path for a user to give you what you need. In the beginning, simpler is almost always better.

Your front door could be as simple as your email address. In a Concierge MVP, your "interface" might be a welcome email that clearly states, "To get started, please reply with the following information..." This is a surprisingly effective and personal way to handle your first few clients.

For a slightly more structured approach, you can use a sophisticated form builder like Typeform or Jotform. These tools allow you to create beautiful, conversational forms that can guide the user through the process of providing inputs, and they can even accept file uploads and payments.

For a more integrated experience that hints at a real product, you can use a simple landing page builder like Carrd or Webflow. You can build a one-page site that explains your service, showcases a testimonial from a pilot user, and has an embedded form as the primary call to action. This provides a professional-looking "front door" without requiring any coding. The key is to make it dead simple for a user to say, "Here is my problem, please solve it."

Layer 2: The "Engine Room" (Your Human-AI Workflow)

This is the core of your service. It is the process by which you transform the customer's input into the valuable output. In your MVP, the "engine" is a hybrid of your own brain, your keyboard, and the specific AI tools you've chosen. This is the workflow from Chapter 9 brought to life, with you acting as the central processing unit.

The key to the MVP engine room is to resist the urge to automate everything at once. Instead, you should document every single manual step you take. Create a checklist for yourself. For the LegalBrief AI example, your internal checklist for fulfilling one order might look like this:

1. Receive document from client via email.

2. Open document and perform a quick scan for any unusual formatting.

3. Copy the entire text of the document.

4. Open my pre-saved prompt in a text file.

5. Go to the AI platform (e.g., OpenAI's Playground, Claude.ai).

6. Paste the prompt and the legal document text into the AI.

7. Run the generation.

8. Copy the AI's output into a new Google Doc.

9. Read through the AI-generated summary, fact-checking it against the original

document and editing for clarity and tone. (This step is critical).

10. Format the Google Doc with the client's name and the date.

11. Export the document as a PDF.

12. Draft a new email to the client.

13. Attach the PDF and send the email.

This checklist is your MVP's source code. It is a precise, repeatable process. By executing it manually, you will quickly discover where the real bottlenecks are. You might find that the AI is great at summarizing but terrible at pulling out specific dates, forcing you to do that part manually. That is a priceless insight that will inform which part of the process you should focus on automating first.

Layer 3: The "Delivery Mechanism" (Delivering the Value)

This is how the customer receives the finished product. Just like the front door, the delivery mechanism for your MVP should be simple, reliable, and professional. In many cases, the best delivery mechanism is a well-written email. It's personal, direct, and allows you to add context or ask for feedback.

You can attach the output directly to the email (e.g., as a PDF report or a CSV file). Alternatively, you can upload the finished product to a cloud storage service like Google Drive or Dropbox and share a link with the customer. This can be useful for larger files and provides a simple way to manage versions if revisions are needed.

For a more product-like feel, you can deliver the results within the same client portal tool we discussed in the case study chapter. A platform like FuseBase or a competitor allows you to create a simple, branded space for each client. You can upload the final report to their portal and the system will automatically notify them. This creates a more professional and centralized experience, making your service feel more like a product and less like a series of emails. The method you choose should align with the level of professionalism and the price point you are aiming for.

Assembling Your First MVP: A Practical Example

Let's walk through the assembly of a new MVP from scratch. Our fictional service is called "PitchCraft AI." Its value proposition is to help startup founders create compelling elevator pitches. The service takes a user's rough notes about their business and transforms them into three well-structured, persuasive pitch paragraphs suitable for an email to an investor.

Step 1: Define the Minimum Service. We will start with a Concierge model. Our promise to the first five customers is: "Send me your brain dump about your business, and I will personally work with my AI tools to craft three killer pitch paragraphs for you within 48 hours."

Step 2: Choose the MVP Components.

Front Door: We will use a simple, free Google Form. It will have one large text box field: "Please describe your business in as much detail as you're comfortable with. Include who your customer is, what problem you solve, and how your solution works." It will also have a field for their email address. We'll link to this Google Form from a basic, one-page website built on Carrd.

Engine Room: Our "engine" is a carefully crafted prompt and a human review process. The prompt, which we've developed through experimentation, might be something like: "You are an expert startup pitch coach. The following is a founder's raw description of their business. Your task is to transform it into three distinct paragraphs for an investor pitch. Paragraph 1 should state the problem and the market. Paragraph 2 should explain the solution and how it works. Paragraph 3 should describe the business model and the team's unique advantage. The tone should be confident, clear, and concise." Our manual checklist involves running this prompt, reviewing the output for quality and accuracy, and performing a round of human edits to perfect the language.

Delivery Mechanism: We will deliver the final three paragraphs in a nicely formatted email. We'll also include a few sentences of personalized commentary, explaining why we chose certain phrasing. This adds a human touch and reinforces the value of the "Concierge" service.

Step 3: Find the First Users. We will reach out to our personal network and post in a few early-stage founder communities, offering to provide this service for free to the first five people who respond, in exchange for a detailed feedback call.

With this simple setup, we can launch our PitchCraft AI MVP in a single afternoon. We haven't written any code. We haven't spent thousands of dollars. But we have a live, functioning service that can deliver real value to a real customer. The learning is about to begin.

From Manual MVP to Scalable Product

The manual MVP is a temporary, but essential, phase. You cannot build a scalable business by personally crafting every single output. The purpose of the manual MVP is to generate the data and revenue needed to justify the next stage of development: gradual automation. Your goal is to systematically replace yourself.

After you have serviced your first ten, twenty, or fifty customers manually, you will have an almost painfully clear understanding of your own workflow. You will know which steps are the most time-consuming, the most repetitive, and the most prone to error. These are your top candidates for automation.

The first level of automation usually involves connecting your existing tools with a workflow automation platform like Zapier or Make. Instead of manually checking your Google Form for new submissions, you can create a "Zap" that is automatically triggered by a new entry. This Zap can take the data from the form and send it directly to the AI model's API, along with your pre-written prompt. The AI's response can then be automatically sent back to you, perhaps by creating a new draft in your Gmail. This simple automation might eliminate five manual steps and save you ten minutes per order.

As your revenue grows, you can continue this process, moving up the chain of automation. The next step might be to replace the Google Form with a more sophisticated front-end that integrates directly with your AI. You might build a simple web application using a no-code tool like Bubble which allows you to create a customer-facing interface that communicates with external APIs. Now, the customer's input can be sent directly to the AI, and the output can be displayed back to them on the screen, all without your intervention.

You will likely find that some steps, particularly the final quality review, are difficult to automate completely. This is where the "human-in-the-loop" model becomes a permanent part of your product. Your goal might not be 100% automation, but 90% automation. Your system handles the entire workflow, but flags certain outputs for a quick human review before they are sent to the customer. This allows you to maintain high quality while still achieving massive operational leverage.

The journey of building an AI business is a journey of iterative automation. You start by being the service. You learn by doing. Then, you methodically teach the machine to replicate your expertise, one step at a time. The MVP is not just the first version of your product; it is the first step on that journey. It is the humble, human-powered seed from which your scalable, AI-driven business will grow.

* * *

14

Customer On-boarding & Experience

The moment a customer clicks "Sign Up" is not the end of a long journey; it is the beginning of a new, even more critical one. You have successfully navigated the treacherous waters of marketing and sales. You have convinced a stranger to give you their email address, their credit card information, and, most importantly, their attention. This is a moment of immense potential and equally immense peril. The next few minutes, hours, and days will determine whether this new user becomes a loyal advocate for your brand or a churn statistic in your analytics dashboard. This fragile, formative period is the domain of customer on-boarding.

On-boarding is the process of systematically guiding a new user from their initial state of hopeful curiosity to a state of confident, successful activation. It is the bridge that connects the promise you made on your landing page to the value delivered inside your application. It is not a single feature, like a product tour, nor is it a simple welcome email. It is the entire, orchestrated experience a customer has from their first login until they achieve the first meaningful outcome with your service, the moment they think, "Aha! This is what I was looking for."

For an AI-based business, a thoughtful on-boarding process is even more essential. You are often asking users to trust a new, sometimes intimidating technology with their data and their workflows. Confusion is your greatest enemy. A user who feels lost or unsure of what to do next will quickly lose confidence and abandon your service. A great on-boarding experience, on the other hand, builds that trust. It demystifies the AI, demonstrates its value quickly, and empowers the user to solve their problem, cementing your service as an indispensable part of their toolkit.

The Goal of On-boarding: Engineering the "Aha!" Moment

Every successful product has what is known as an "aha!" moment. It is the point in the user experience where the value proposition clicks into place in the user's mind. It's the moment of sudden, satisfying realization. For Facebook, it was when a user found and connected with a handful of their real-life friends. For Dropbox, it was when a user saved a file on their desktop and saw it magically appear on their phone. The user moves from understanding the product conceptually to feeling its value emotionally.

The singular goal of your on-boarding process is to guide the user to their "aha!" moment as quickly and frictionlessly as possible. Everything else is secondary. To do this, you must first define what that moment is for your specific service. This requires you to look beyond your features and focus on the customer's desired outcome. The "aha!" moment is not when they see your beautiful dashboard; it is when that dashboard gives them an insight that saves them an hour of work.

Let's consider our fictional "Insight AI" research assistant service. What is its "aha!" moment? It is not when the user successfully fills out the research request form. It is not when they receive the confirmation email. The "aha!" moment is when they open the first AI-generated report and see a complex topic distilled into a clear, insightful summary, saving them hours of manual research. The entire on-boarding process must be reverse-engineered from this moment. Every step, every email, every instruction should be designed to propel the user toward that specific, value-laden experience.

Identifying your "aha!" moment requires you to answer a critical question: What is the minimum set of actions a user must perform to experience the core value of your product? For Insight AI, it's submitting one research topic. For ClientFlow AI, it might be creating one client portal and uploading one document. For an AI transcription service, it's uploading one audio file and getting back an accurate transcript. This core action path is the spine of your on-boarding journey.

From Ad-Hoc to Architected: Mapping the Ideal User Journey

In the earliest days of your MVP, your on-boarding process was likely a manual, concierge-style service. You personally guided each user through the setup via emails and phone calls. This was an invaluable learning experience, but it is not scalable. To grow, you must translate the lessons from those manual interactions into a structured, repeatable, and largely automated journey. This means mapping out the ideal sequence of steps a user takes from signup to activation.

Start with a whiteboard or a blank document and chart the user's path. The journey begins before they even log in for the first time. It starts with the Welcome Email. This is your first opportunity to set the tone and guide their expectations. A single, well-crafted email can make the difference between a user who logs in immediately and one who forgets they ever signed up.

Once they log in, you must define the First-Run Experience. What is the very first thing a new user should see and do? Do not dump them onto a blank, empty dashboard. An empty screen is intimidating and creates a sense of "now what?". Instead, the first-run experience should be a guided path to their first small win. This could be a setup wizard that walks them through a few critical configuration steps or a pre-populated sample project that demonstrates what the final output looks like.

The next phase of the journey involves identifying the key Activation Events. These are the critical actions that your most successful users take early in their lifecycle. You can discover these by analyzing the behavior of your pilot users. Did all of your happy, paying customers connect their Google account within the first day? Did they all create their first project within the first session? These actions are strong indicators of future retention. Your on-boarding process should be explicitly designed to encourage all new users to complete these specific events.

Finally, the journey map should account for Ongoing Education. On-boarding doesn't stop after the first day. How will you introduce users to more advanced features over time? This can be accomplished through a "drip" email sequence that sends a new tip each week, or through in-app notifications that highlight a useful feature they haven't tried yet. This gradual education helps users get progressively more value out of your service, increasing its stickiness and reducing churn.

The Building Blocks of a Modern On-boarding Experience

With your ideal journey mapped out, you can now choose the tools and tactics to build it. A great on-boarding experience is a symphony of different components working together to create a seamless and supportive environment for the new user.

The Welcome Sequence: Your First Impression

The moment a user signs up, a welcome email should be sent automatically. This is non-negotiable. This first email should do three things:

1. Confirm the Action: Reassure the user that their signup was successful.

2. State the Value: Briefly reiterate the primary benefit they are about to receive.

3. Provide a Clear Next Step: Give them a single, obvious call to action, usually a button

that says "Log In and Get Started" or "Create Your First Report."

But don't stop at one email. A welcome "sequence" or "drip campaign" is far more effective. This is a series of three to five automated emails sent over the user's first week. Each email has a single, focused purpose.

Email 1 (Day 0): The welcome and call to action.

Email 2 (Day 1): A practical tip for getting started, focusing on the first key activation

event.

Email 3 (Day 3): A link to a case study or testimonial showing how another customer l

like them found success. This provides social proof and inspiration.

Email 4 (Day 5): A personal check-in from the founder (which can still be automated)

asking if they have any questions. This builds a human connection.

Tools like Mailchimp, ConvertKit, or Customer.io make it easy to build these automated sequences without writing any code.

The First Login: Guided Tours and Interactive Checklists

The first time a user logs into your application is a make-or-break moment. You need to hold their hand and guide them. A common approach is a Product Tour a series of pop-up tooltips that point to different elements of the user interface. While these can be helpful, they are often misused. A tour that explains every single button on the screen is overwhelming and will be quickly dismissed. A good tour is short, focused, and drives the user to take a single, valuable action.

A more effective modern alternative is the Interactive Checklist. When the user logs in, they are presented with a small checklist of two to four key setup tasks. For example: "1. Create your first project. 2. Invite a team member. 3. Connect your account to Slack." As the user completes each task, the item is checked off. This technique leverages a powerful psychological principle called the Zeigarnik effect, which states that people have a better memory for uncompleted tasks. The open checklist creates a gentle but persistent motivation for the user to finish the setup process.

There are many third-party tools like Appcue, Userguiding, or Intercom that allow you to build these sophisticated in-app tours and checklists without needing to be a developer. They provide visual editors that let you design and deploy these on-boarding flows directly on top of your existing application.

The Self-Service Safety Net: The Knowledge Base

No matter how good your guided on-boarding is, users will always have questions. You cannot be available to answer every one of them personally. A comprehensive, well-organized Knowledge Base or Help Center is your self-service support solution. This is a centralized repository of "how-to" articles, video tutorials, and answers to frequently asked questions (FAQs).

Building this knowledge base should not be a daunting task. Start with the questions your pilot users asked you. Every time a user asks a question, it's a signal that your product isn't clear enough and that an article is needed. Write a clear answer to that question, take a few screenshots, and publish it. Over time, you will build a rich library of content that empowers users to find answers on their own. This not only improves the customer experience but also dramatically reduces your future customer support workload. Platforms like Zendesk, Help Scout, or even a simple FuseBase portal make it easy to create and manage a professional-looking help center.

AI as Your On-boarding Concierge

As an AI-based business, you have a unique opportunity to "eat your own dog food" and use AI to create a smarter, more personalized on-boarding experience. Instead of a static, one-size-fits-all process, you can use AI agents to act as a personal concierge for every new user, guiding them in a way that is tailored to their specific needs.

Personalized On-boarding at Scale

The personalization can begin before the user even sees the product. During the sign-up process, you can ask one or two simple questions about their role or their primary goal. "What is your role? (e.g., Solo Founder, Agency Marketer, Project Manager)" or "What is the main thing you want to accomplish with our service?". This data can then be used to dynamically customize the on-boarding experience.

An AI workflow can take these inputs and generate a personalized welcome email. A founder might receive an email that emphasizes time-saving benefits, while an agency marketer receives one that highlights features for managing multiple clients. The in-app checklist they see on first login could also be customized. The founder might see a task to "Draft your first investor pitch," while the marketer sees "Create your first client campaign." This makes the user feel like the product was designed specifically for them.

Interactive AI Guides

Your knowledge base is a powerful asset, but it is a passive one. A user has to leave what they are doing and go search for an answer. You can bring this knowledge to life by embedding an AI-powered assistant directly within your application. This agent can be trained exclusively on your help center articles and product documentation.

When a new user has a question, they don't have to go anywhere. They can simply open a chat widget and ask in plain English, "How do I add my company's logo to a report?". The AI agent, having studied your knowledge base, can provide an immediate, contextual answer. This is infinitely better than forcing a user to hunt through dozens of articles. This technology, similar to what we discussed in the FuseBase case study, can be a game-changer for user on-boarding, providing instant, 24/7 support at a fraction of the cost of a human team.

Proactive Assistance

The most advanced use of AI in on-boarding is to be proactive, not just reactive. You can design workflows that monitor user behavior and automatically intervene when it looks like a user is stuck. For example, your system can detect that a new user has started the process of creating their first project but hasn't completed it after 48 hours. This is a red flag for potential churn.

Instead of waiting for the user to complain, your workflow can trigger a proactive, helpful intervention. An AI agent could send an automated email that says, "Hi John, I noticed you started creating a project but haven't finished yet. Sometimes connecting to an external data source can be tricky. Here's a 2-minute video that walks you through it. Can I help with anything?" This kind of proactive outreach feels incredibly personal and helpful, and it can be the nudge a user needs to get over a hurdle and back on the path to success.

Measuring Success: Are They On Board?

A beautifully designed on-boarding process is worthless if it doesn't actually work. You must measure its effectiveness with cold, hard data. Tracking a few key performance indicators (KPIs) will tell you whether your efforts are paying off and where you need to improve.

The first and most important metric is Time to Value (TTV). This is the average time it takes for a new user to reach their "aha!" moment. You should be relentlessly focused on reducing this number. If it takes a user three weeks to experience the core value of your product, most of them will be long gone before they get there. Every change you make to your on-boarding should be judged against the question: "Will this help a user get to their 'aha!' moment faster?"

Next is the Activation Rate. This is the percentage of new users who complete your key activation events within a specific timeframe (e.g., the first seven days). If you've identified that inviting a team member is a critical step for retention, you need to track what percentage of new accounts actually do it. A low activation rate is a clear sign that there is too much friction in your on-boarding process for that specific step.

You should also keep a close eye on your User Churn Rate specifically in the first 30 days. If a high percentage of your users are canceling their subscriptions in the first month, it's an almost certain indicator that your on-boarding is failing. They are signing up based on the promise of your marketing but are not successfully finding that value within the product itself.

Finally, the number of Support Tickets from New Users is a direct measure of your on-boarding's clarity. If your support team is constantly being flooded with the same basic setup questions, it means your in-app guidance and your knowledge base are not doing their job effectively. Each support ticket is a gift of feedback, pointing you directly to a source of user confusion that needs to be fixed.

By combining these quantitative metrics with the qualitative feedback you get from talking to your users, you can create a powerful feedback loop. You can see what is happening in your numbers and understand why it is happening from your conversations. This allows you to treat your on-boarding not as a project to be completed, but as a product to be continuously improved, ensuring every new customer has the best possible chance of becoming a lifelong fan.

* * *

15

Managing Data & Privacy in AI Startups

In the traditional world of business, data was often the exhaust, a digital byproduct of a transaction or an interaction, filed away for accounting or later analysis. In the world of artificial intelligence, this relationship is inverted. Data is not the exhaust; it is the fuel. It is the raw ore from which your AI models learn, the context they use to make decisions, and the lifeblood of the service you provide. How you collect, manage, protect, and use this fuel is not a secondary operational detail. It is a central, strategic function that will define your company's potential, its reputation, and its very survival.

Many founders view data privacy and management as a legal chore, a bureaucratic hurdle to be cleared with a boilerplate privacy policy and a sigh of resignation. This is a profound misunderstanding of its importance. For an AI business, your approach to data is a core part of your product and a fundamental pillar of your brand. In an age of increasing skepticism about technology and a constant drumbeat of news about data breaches, demonstrating trustworthy stewardship of customer data is not a defensive measure; it is a powerful competitive advantage.

Customers, both individuals and businesses, are becoming increasingly sophisticated about their data. They want to know what you are collecting, why you are collecting it, and how it is being used. A company that is evasive or unclear on these points instantly raises red flags. A company that is transparent, respectful, and puts the user in control builds a foundation of trust that can be a far more durable moat than any single technical feature. This chapter is your guide to building that foundation, moving beyond the legal boilerplate to create a data and privacy strategy that is not only compliant but also a core reason customers choose you.

The New Data Equation: Inputs, Outputs, and Training Sets

To manage data effectively in an AI business, you first need to understand the different forms it takes. Your data is not a single, monolithic entity. It flows through your system in various states, each with its own set of privacy implications and management requirements. Thinking in terms of these categories will help you create clearer policies and more secure systems.

The most obvious category is User-Provided Input. This is the data that your customers actively give you to get a result. It's the audio file they upload for transcription, the legal document they submit for summarization, or the raw business metrics they provide for analysis. This data is often highly sensitive, confidential, and is the property of your customer. It has been entrusted to you for a specific purpose, and its protection is your highest obligation.

Next is the AI-Generated Output. This is the result your service produces after processing the user's input. It's the finished transcript, the summarized brief, or the analytics report. The ownership and privacy of this output can be a complex question. While it was generated by your system, it is derived directly from the user's input. Your Terms of Service must be crystal clear about who owns this output. In most cases, for a B2B service, the output is considered the work product and property of the customer who paid for it.

The third, and most sensitive, category is Training Data. This is the information used to teach your AI models how to perform their tasks. This can include publicly available datasets, data you've licensed, or, most controversially, data derived from your own users' activity. How you handle the relationship between user-provided inputs and your training data is one of the most critical ethical and legal decisions you will make. It's a decision that requires a deliberate strategy, not a casual assumption.

Finally, there is System and Usage Metadata. This is the data about how your customers use your service. It includes information like how often they log in, which features they use most, how long it takes an AI to process their requests, and which parts of your interface they click on. This data is invaluable for improving your product and on-boarding flows, but it is still customer data and must be treated with respect, made anonymous when possible, and explained clearly in your privacy policy.

The Bedrock Principles of Data Stewardship

Before diving into specific regulations or technologies, it's essential to internalize a few core principles that should govern every decision you make about data. These are not legal rules but philosophical commitments. Building your business on this bedrock will make compliance with specific laws much easier down the road, as you will have already adopted the spirit of the law.

The first principle is Data Minimization. This is the simple but powerful idea that you should only collect the data you absolutely need to provide your service. The more data you collect, the greater your responsibility and the larger your "attack surface" for a potential breach. It can be tempting to ask for dozens of data points during sign-up, thinking you might use them later for marketing. Resist this temptation. If you don't need a user's phone number to deliver your service, don't ask for it. This discipline not only reduces your risk but also builds trust by demonstrating that you are respectful of the user's time and privacy.

The second principle is Purpose Limitation. This means you should only use the data you collect for the specific purpose you told the user you were collecting it for. If a user uploads a confidential document to be summarized, that is the only purpose for which that document should be used. Using it for any other purpose, such as adding it to a global database to train a new AI model, without their explicit consent, is a violation of trust and, in many jurisdictions, a violation of the law.

This leads directly to the third principle: Radical Transparency. You must be honest and clear with your users about your data practices. Your Privacy Policy should not be a 30-page document of impenetrable legalese designed to be ignored. It should be a clear, concise, and human-readable explanation of what you collect, why you collect it, and what you do with it. Many modern companies supplement their formal legal policy with a plain-English summary or an FAQ section. This transparency isn't just about compliance; it's about treating your users as intelligent partners rather than subjects to be harvested for data.

The Most Dangerous Question: Using Customer Data to Train Your AI

For any AI founder, the temptation is immense. You have a stream of real-world data coming from your users. Using this data to continuously fine-tune and improve your AI models could make your product smarter, more accurate, and more valuable. It could be your key competitive advantage. It could also be the decision that destroys your company.

Using customer data for model training is the single most sensitive data privacy issue for an AI startup. If handled improperly, it can lead to devastating breaches of confidentiality, legal penalties, and a complete collapse of customer trust. If you are even considering this path, you must proceed with extreme caution and a commitment to ethical practices.

There are several ways to approach this, ranging from the safe to the highly risky. The gold standard, and the only truly defensible approach, is to get Explicit, Opt-In Consent. This means you do not use any customer data for training by default. Instead, you explicitly ask them for permission. This cannot be a pre-checked box hidden in your Terms of Service. It should be a clear, separate request.

You might present it in the user's account settings with a toggle switch and a clear explanation: "Help improve [Your Product] for everyone? Allow us to use an anonymized version of your data to train our AI models. We will never use your personal information and this will help us make the service smarter and more accurate. [Learn More]." By making it an opt-in choice, you put the user in control and ensure that anyone whose data you use for training has given you their knowing and enthusiastic permission.

Another approach is to rely on Anonymization and Aggregation. The idea is to strip out all Personally Identifiable Information (PII), names, email addresses, locations, company names, from the data before it is added to a training set. While this is a necessary step, it is not a silver bullet. Researchers have repeatedly shown that it is possible to "de-anonymize" datasets by cross-referencing them with other sources. True anonymization is incredibly difficult to achieve, and you should not assume that simply removing a few obvious fields makes the data safe.

Given these risks, many of the most successful and trustworthy AI companies adopt the simplest and safest policy of all: a strict firewall. They make a public commitment that customer data is sacrosanct. It is used only to provide the service to that specific customer and is never, under any circumstances, used for model training. While this may seem like you are giving up a potential advantage, you are gaining something far more valuable: a powerful marketing message built on trust. Being able to state unequivocally on your website, "We will never train our models on your private data," can be a massive differentiator that attracts security-conscious customers, especially in the B2B space.

Building Your Data Fortress: An Introduction to Security

While privacy is about the rules of engagement for how you use data, security is about the practical measures you take to protect it from unauthorized access. For a startup, you don't need to become a cybersecurity expert, but you do need to understand and implement a few non-negotiable security fundamentals from day one.

The first line of defense is Access Control. Not everyone in your company needs access to raw customer data. The "Principle of Least Privilege" dictates that an employee should only have access to the specific data and systems they need to do their job. Your marketing intern does not need access to the production database. Implement role-based access controls in your systems to enforce this. The fewer people who can access sensitive data, the smaller the risk of an accidental leak or a malicious breach.

Next is Encryption. This is the process of scrambling data so it can only be read by someone with the correct key. Encryption is not optional; it is a baseline requirement. Your data must be encrypted in two states. It must be encrypted in transit which means using HTTPS (the padlock icon in your browser) for all communication between your user and your servers. It must also be encrypted at rest which means the data is scrambled while it is stored on your database servers. Most modern cloud providers and database services offer these features as standard, but you must ensure they are enabled and configured correctly.

Your security is only as strong as the weakest link in your supply chain. When you choose your third-party tools, your AI platform provider, your cloud host, your CRM, you are entrusting them with your customers' data. You must perform Vendor Security Diligence. Look for vendors who take security seriously. Do they have industry-standard security certifications, such as SOC 2 or ISO 27001? These certifications are independent audits that verify a company has robust security controls in place. Choosing vendors with these credentials shows your customers that you have done your homework.

Finally, you must establish a Data Retention Policy. You should not store customer data forever. The longer you hold onto data, the more liability you carry. Your policy should define how long you need to keep data for legitimate business purposes and should mandate its secure deletion after that period. For example, your policy might state that all data associated with a customer account will be permanently deleted 90 days after the account is closed. This minimizes your risk and respects the user's "right to be forgotten."

The Regulatory Landscape: A Founder's Guide to the Alphabet Soup

The world of data privacy is governed by a growing number of complex regulations. While you should consult a lawyer for specific advice, you need to be aware of the major laws that will likely impact your business. The good news is that if you adopt the core principles of data minimization, purpose limitation, and transparency, you will be well on your way to complying with most of them.

The most significant of these is Europe's General Data Protection Regulation (GDPR). Even if you are not based in the EU, GDPR applies to you if you offer your services to or process the data of people located in the EU. GDPR grants individuals a strong set of rights over their data, including the right to access the data a company holds on them, the right to correct inaccuracies, and the right to request its deletion. Fines for non-compliance can be astronomical, up to 4% of a company's global annual revenue.

In the United States, the most prominent state-level law is the California Consumer Privacy Act (CCPA) as amended by the California Privacy Rights

Act (CPRA). It grants California residents similar rights to those in GDPR, such as the right to know what personal information is being collected about them and the right to opt-out of the sale or sharing of that information. Other states are rapidly following suit with their own privacy laws.

The key takeaway for a founder is not to become an expert on every clause of every law. It is to recognize that the global trend is toward strengthening individual privacy rights. The most strategic approach is to adopt a policy of "Privacy by Design." This means you don't try to bolt on privacy features after the fact. You build your product and your business processes from the very beginning with the strictest privacy standards in mind. Assume your users are from Europe and California. Build systems that make it easy for you to respond to data access or deletion requests. By designing for the highest standard, you future-proof your business against the next wave of regulations.

Privacy as a Product Feature

In the final analysis, your approach to data and privacy should not be seen as a cost center to be minimized or a legal risk to be managed. It should be seen as an opportunity to be seized. In a crowded marketplace, trust can be your most potent differentiator. You can and should market your privacy practices as a core feature of your product.

Create a dedicated "Trust Center" or "Security" page on your website. On this page, use plain English to explain your commitment to protecting customer data. Detail your security measures like encryption and access controls. State your position on using customer data for training clearly and proudly. Link to your SOC 2 report if you have one.

This kind of transparency does more than just reassure security-conscious customers. It sends a powerful signal about the character of your company. It says that you see your customers as partners to be respected, not as resources to be exploited. It says that you are building a business for the long term, on a foundation of integrity. In the age of AI, where the relationship between technology and humanity is being redefined, there are few assets more valuable than that.

* * *

16

Integrating No-Code & Low-Code Solutions

You've built your first Minimum Viable Product. It might have been a high-touch concierge service, a clever Wizard of Oz setup, or a combination of the two. You have serviced your first handful of users, likely with a frantic, manual process of copying data between browser tabs, running AI prompts, and pasting results into an email. You have learned an incredible amount, but you have also felt the sharp pain of inefficiency. This manual process is your business's training wheels; it has provided stability and invaluable learning, but it is not built for speed. To grow, you must take the training wheels off.

This is the moment where you evolve from a founder who uses tools into a founder who connects them. Your business is not a single piece of software; it is a stack, an ecosystem of specialized applications working in concert. Your customer relationship manager (CRM) needs to talk to your payment processor. Your form builder needs to talk to your AI model. Your AI model needs to talk to your project management tool. This chapter is about building the digital nervous system that allows these disparate parts to communicate and operate as a single, cohesive, automated engine.

We are moving beyond the conceptual workflow design from Chapter 9 and into the practical, nuts-and-bolts reality of integration. This is the domain of no-code and low-code solutions, the digital glue that holds a modern startup together. It's where you will systematically replace your own manual copy-pasting with automated data flows, freeing you from the role of a human API. By mastering these connections, you can build a service that is not only powerful but also scalable, reliable, and ready for growth.

Your Business as a Tech Stack

It is a common misconception that to build a technology business, you must build all the technology yourself. The modern reality is that you are an architect, not a bricklayer. Your job is to select the best pre-fabricated components from a vast marketplace of Software-as-a-Service (SaaS) tools and assemble them into a unique and valuable solution. No single no-code platform can do everything you need. You will inevitably find that the best tool for building a landing page is different from the best tool for managing a customer database, which is different from the best tool for running a specific AI task.

Your competitive advantage comes not from building a better CRM from scratch, but from creating a novel way to connect an existing CRM to a powerful AI agent to deliver a new kind of service. This assembly of tools is your tech stack. A typical stack for a new AI service business might include a form builder like Typeform for data intake, a database like Airtable for managing customer information, an AI platform like OpenAI or Anthropic for the core processing, a client portal like FuseBase for delivery, and a payment processor like Stripe to handle billing.

On their own, these are just isolated islands of functionality. The magic, and the automation, happens when you build bridges between them. An integration is a bridge that allows data to flow automatically from one application to another. When a new form is submitted in Typeform, an integration can automatically create a new customer record in Airtable. This is the first step in replacing your manual workload with a reliable, automated process.

The Conductors of the Orchestra: Integration Platforms

While some applications have direct, built-in connections to each other (often called "native integrations"), it is impossible for every app to connect to every other app. This is where a category of tools known as iPaaS (Integration Platform as a Service) comes in. These platforms are the master conductors of your no-code orchestra. They are universal translators, designed with one purpose: to listen for events in one application and trigger actions in another.

The most well-known players in this space are Zapier and Make (formerly Integromat). Think of them as digital switchboard operators. You don't need to know how the phone lines are wired; you just need to tell the operator, "When a call comes in from this number, please connect it to that extension." In practice, you build simple "if this, then that" recipes. In Zapier, these are called "Zaps." In Make, they are called "Scenarios." The logic is the same.

A simple Zap might be: "When I receive a new email in Gmail with 'Invoice' in the subject line (the trigger), automatically save the attachment to a specific folder in my Google Drive (the action)." This simple automation, which takes about five minutes to set up, can save you hours of administrative drudgery over the course of a year. For your AI business, these recipes will be more sophisticated, involving multiple steps and multiple tools, forming the backbone of your automated workflow.

These platforms are the key to unlocking the true potential of your tech stack. They allow you to connect best-in-class tools, creating a system that is far more powerful and flexible than what any single, all-in-one platform could offer. They are the essential ingredient for moving from a series of manual tasks to a cohesive, automated service.

APIs and Webhooks: A Simple Guide for Non-Engineers

To use integration platforms effectively, you need a basic conceptual understanding of two terms that often intimidate non-technical founders: API and Webhook. You do not need to know how to code them, but understanding what they do will demystify the entire process of integration and empower you to build much more sophisticated workflows.

An API (Application Programming Interface) is best understood as a menu of actions that a software application makes available to the outside world. Imagine you walk into a restaurant. You can't just go into the kitchen and start cooking. Instead, you are handed a menu. The menu lists a specific set of items the kitchen is prepared to make for you (e.g., create a new customer, update a record, find a specific piece of information). You give your order to the waiter (the API call), the waiter takes it to the kitchen, and the kitchen sends back your prepared dish (the data).

When you use a tool like Zapier to connect to Airtable, Zapier is using Airtable's API, its "menu", to perform actions like "Create a New Record" or "Update a Record." An API is how one program tells another program what to do.

A Webhook serves a different but complementary purpose. If an API is like ordering from a menu, a webhook is like a package delivery notification. Instead of you having to constantly call the delivery company and ask, "Is my package here yet?" (a process called "polling"), the delivery company sends you an automated message the moment the package arrives at your door.

In the software world, a webhook is an automated notification sent from one app to another whenever a specific event occurs. When a customer makes a successful payment in Stripe, Stripe can send a webhook notification, a small packet of data saying, "This person just paid this amount for this product", to a specific URL. Your integration platform can "listen" at that URL, catch that notification, and use it as a trigger for a workflow. Webhooks are incredibly efficient and powerful because they enable real-time automation. They are the "when this happens" part of your "if this, then that" recipe.

A Multi-Tool Workflow in Action

Let's bring this down to earth with a concrete example. We'll design an automated workflow for a fictional service called "PodScribe AI," which provides podcasters with AI-generated transcripts and show notes.

Our stack consists of:
Dropbox: for file submission.
AssemblyAI: a powerful AI model for audio transcription.
OpenAI's GPT-4: for generating show notes from the transcript.
Airtable: to act as our central project management database.
Gmail: for final delivery to the client.

Our iPaaS tool of choice will be Make because its visual, flowchart-style interface is excellent for visualizing multi-step workflows.

Step 1: The Trigger. The entire workflow begins when our podcast client uploads a new MP3 audio file to a specific, shared Dropbox folder. In Make, we set up our first module: "Watch Files in a Folder" in Dropbox. This module will check the folder every 15 minutes for new files.

Step 2: First AI Action (Transcription). When a new file is detected, the workflow is triggered. The Dropbox module passes the audio file to the next module, which is an integration with AssemblyAI. We configure this module to take the incoming file and submit it for transcription. Because transcription can take a few minutes, this module will wait until the job is complete before proceeding.

Step 3: Data Formatting. The output from AssemblyAI is a huge block of text, the full transcript. Before we can use it, we might need to clean it up slightly. We can use a simple text formatting module within Make to ensure it's in a clean, readable format for the next AI.

Step 4: Second AI Action (Summarization). The cleaned transcript is now passed as an input to the next module, which is an integration with OpenAI. Here, we craft a detailed prompt, similar to the ones we've discussed in previous chapters: "You are a helpful podcast production assistant. The following is a transcript of a podcast episode. Please generate the following: 1. A one-paragraph summary of the episode. 2. A bulleted list of the 5 key takeaways. 3. Three potential titles for the episode."

Step 5: Centralizing Data. The structured output from OpenAI (the summary, takeaways, and titles) is then passed to the next module: an integration with Airtable. We configure this module to "Create a New Record" in our "Podcast Episodes" base. We map the data from OpenAI to the corresponding fields in Airtable: the summary goes into the "Summary" field, the takeaways go into the "Takeaways" field, and so on.

Step 6: Final Delivery. The last module in our scenario is an integration with Gmail. We configure this module to "Send an Email." The recipient is our client's email address (which we can store in Airtable). The subject line can be dynamic: "Show Notes for [Original Filename] are Ready!". The body of the email can be populated with the data from the Airtable record, presenting the show notes in a clean, professional format.

What we have just built is a fully automated assembly line. A task that would have taken a human an hour or more of manual work is now completed automatically, triggered by a simple file upload. This is the power of integrating no-code and low-code solutions.

The Low-Code Leap: When a Little Code Goes a Long Way

As you build more sophisticated workflows, you will eventually encounter a problem that a purely no-code, drag-and-drop interface cannot solve. You might need to perform a custom calculation, reformat a date in a specific way, or parse a complex piece of data before sending it to the next tool. This is where you will take your first small step into the world of low-code.

This does not mean you need to become a software developer. The "code" in low-code is often just a single line, a simple formula in a spreadsheet, a snippet of JavaScript to transform some text, or a bit of HTML to format an email. Most integration platforms have built-in "Code" or "Formula" modules that allow you to inject these small snippets of logic directly into your workflow.

For example, imagine your AI tool returns a person's name as "John Smith", but you want to address them in an email as just "John". A purely no-code tool might not have a simple way to do this. A low-code approach would involve adding a small JavaScript module to your workflow that takes the full name as an input and runs a simple function to split the text at the space and return only the first part. Learning these tiny bits of code can give you superpowers, allowing you to overcome the limitations of the standard modules and customize your workflows with much greater precision.

Another common low-code scenario involves working directly with an application's API when your integration platform doesn't have a pre-built module for it. If you find a new AI tool that you want to use, but Zapier or Make don't have a native integration, you are not necessarily stuck. As long as that tool has a documented API, you can use a generic "HTTP Request" or "API Call" module. This involves a bit more configuration, you will have to copy and paste the API endpoint URL from the tool's documentation and structure the data you send in a format called JSON (JavaScript Object Notation). While this looks intimidating at first, it is often just a matter of careful reading and matching the format shown in the documentation. This skill opens up a vastly larger universe of tools for you to integrate into your stack.

Building for Resilience: Debugging Your Stack

A system built from five different cloud services connected by an integration platform is an incredibly powerful thing. It is also a system with five potential points of failure. When your workflow breaks, and it will, you need a systematic way to figure out what went wrong. Debugging a no-code stack is a crucial operational skill.

Your first and best tool is the run history within your iPaaS platform. Tools like Zapier and Make keep a detailed log of every time a workflow runs. When an error occurs, this log is your crime scene. You can inspect the data that came into each module and the data that went out. This allows you to trace the problem step by step.

Did the trigger fire correctly? If not, the problem is with the connection to your first app. Did the data get passed correctly from Step 1 to Step 2? If the data in Step 2 looks wrong, the issue lies in the transformation happening in Step 1. Did Step 3 produce an error? The log will often show you the exact error message returned by that application's API, which can give you a clear clue as to what went wrong (e.g., "Invalid API Key," "Missing Required Field").

Your troubleshooting process should be one of isolation. Temporarily disable parts of your workflow to see if the rest runs correctly. Test each module's connection independently. Often, the problem is as simple as a password you changed in one application that you forgot to update in your integration platform, breaking the connection. By approaching debugging with a calm, methodical process of elimination, you can quickly diagnose and fix issues, ensuring your automated engine keeps running smoothly.

This ability to stitch together disparate systems, to act as the architect of your own custom tech stack, is one of the defining skills of the modern founder. You are no longer limited by your ability to write code. You are only limited by your ability to understand a problem and creatively assemble the right set of tools to solve it. This is the practical, hands-on work that turns a brilliant idea into a scalable, automated, and ultimately successful AI business.

* * *

17

Effective Content Creation With AI

Content is the currency of the modern internet. It is the language you use to attract an audience, the evidence you provide to build trust, and the story you tell to convince a customer that you understand their world. For a new business, creating a steady stream of high-quality content, blog posts, social media updates, case studies, newsletters, has traditionally been a monumental task, a voracious consumer of time and resources. It often feels like a choice between building your product and talking about your product. Today, artificial intelligence has fundamentally altered this equation.

The emergence of powerful generative AI models has transformed content creation from a purely artisanal craft into a streamlined, scalable production process. The bottleneck of the blank page, the hours spent on research, and the friction of drafting can be dramatically reduced, allowing a solo founder or a small team to generate the output of a much larger marketing department. This is not about abdicating your responsibility or outsourcing your voice to a machine. It is about augmentation.

Effective content creation with AI is not about pushing a button and publishing whatever the machine spits out. That is a recipe for generic, soulless content that repels rather than attracts. Instead, it's about learning to wield AI as a powerful co-pilot, a tireless research assistant, and an infinitely patient brainstorming partner. Your role shifts from being the manual laborer of content creation to being the strategist, the editor, and the final arbiter of quality. This chapter will provide a framework for this new way of working, showing you how to build a content engine that is not only efficient but also effective at building your brand and growing your business.

From Creative Act to Production Workflow

The first mental shift required to leverage AI effectively is to stop thinking of content creation as a singular, mystical act of inspiration and start thinking of it as a repeatable, multi-stage workflow. Like any manufacturing process, it has distinct phases, each with its own inputs and outputs. By breaking down the process, you can identify precisely where to inject AI to gain the most leverage. The five key stages of this new content assembly line are: Ideation, Research, Drafting, Editing, and Repurposing.

Your role as the founder is to manage this assembly line. You define the strategy, set the quality standards at each stage, and provide the critical human touch that turns a generic draft into a valuable asset. The AI acts as your specialized workforce, executing specific tasks at each stage with incredible speed. This systematic approach allows you to move beyond creating a single piece of content and start building a true content engine, a reliable system that produces a predictable output of high-quality marketing materials week after week. This consistency is what builds an audience and drives growth over time.

Stage One: AI as Your Unslump Machine

Every piece of content begins with an idea. For many, this is the most difficult stage; a staring contest with a blinking cursor on a blank screen. AI excels at breaking this creative logjam. It can act as an infinite source of inspiration, generating a vast number of potential ideas that you can then curate and refine. Your job is not to come up with the perfect idea from scratch, but to ask the AI the right questions to uncover promising directions.

Start by feeding the AI the context of your business. Remind it of your Ideal Customer Profile and their core problems. A powerful prompt might be: "I am creating content for my AI service, ClientFlow AI. My target audience is founders of small consulting firms with 5-50 employees. Their biggest pain points are disorganized client on-boarding, wasting non-billable hours on administrative tasks, and appearing unprofessional to new clients. Generate 20 compelling blog post titles that would grab their attention and address these specific pains." The AI might return ideas like "The On-boarding Mistake That's Costing Your Consultancy Clients" or "5 Ways to Automate Your Client Intake Before You Hire an Assistant."

You can also use AI for competitive analysis. Find three or four popular articles written by competitors or industry publications on a topic you want to cover. Feed the text of these articles to the AI and ask: "Given these articles on client management, what important angles or sub-topics have been overlooked? What questions might a reader still have after reading these?" This technique uses the AI to find the gaps in the existing conversation, allowing you to create content that is more comprehensive and original.

Finally, AI can be a powerful tool for search engine optimization (SEO) research. You can ask it to brainstorm long-tail keywords, the longer, more specific search phrases that indicate a user is closer to a buying decision. "Generate a list of 50 long-tail keywords a consulting firm owner might use when they are looking for a solution to their messy client on-boarding process." The AI will generate a list you can use to inform your content titles and headings, increasing the likelihood that your target audience will discover your content through Google. At this stage, your role is that of a prospector, sifting through the many ideas the AI unearths to find the few nuggets of gold that perfectly align with your GTM strategy.

Stage Two: AI as Your Instant Research Assistant

Once you have a compelling topic, the next step is to gather the information and structure your argument. Traditionally, this involved hours of searching, reading, and synthesizing information from dozens of sources. An AI can compress this research phase from hours into minutes. It can act as a tireless assistant that reads and summarizes vast amounts of text, helping you build a strong foundation for your content.

If you find a long, dense industry report or academic study that is relevant to your topic, you don't need to read every word. You can provide the text to an AI and ask for a summary. "Please summarize the key findings of the following report on small business efficiency in five bullet points." This allows you to quickly extract the most salient information and decide if it's worth a deeper dive.

More importantly, you can use the AI to create a detailed structure for your content before you write a single sentence of prose. A well-structured outline is the blueprint for a great article. Give the AI your chosen title and ask it to build this blueprint for you. "Create a detailed outline for a blog post titled 'The 5 Hidden Costs of a Messy Client On-boarding Process.' The outline should include a short introduction, a section for each of the five costs with three sub-bullets explaining the point, and a concluding section that briefly introduces our product as a solution."

The AI will generate a logical, well-organized structure that you can then use to guide the drafting process. This outlining step is critical because it forces you to think through your argument before you start writing. It ensures your final piece will be coherent and easy for a reader to follow. You can even ask the AI to find relevant statistics to support your points, but with a crucial caveat: you must treat any statistic generated by an AI as a lead, not a fact. Always follow up and find the original source to verify its accuracy and context.

Stage Three: Crafting the AI-Assisted First Draft

This is the stage that has captured the most public attention. With your idea and your outline in hand, you can now instruct the AI to write the first draft of your content. The quality of this draft will be a direct reflection of the quality of your instructions. A lazy, one-sentence prompt will yield a generic, unusable result. A detailed, context-rich prompt will produce a surprisingly sophisticated starting point. This is the skill of prompt engineering for content creation.

A great prompt for drafting content has several key components. First, assign the AI a Role. "Act as a world-class B2B content marketer with deep expertise in the consulting industry." This primes the model to adopt a specific style and knowledge base.

Second, provide deep Context. This includes the outline you just created, your target audience persona, and your brand voice. "You are writing for consulting firm founders who are time-poor and pragmatic. Our brand voice is: helpful, confident, and professional, but not stuffy or academic. Use clear, simple language."

Third, give specific Instructions on format and style. "Write an introduction based on the first section of the outline. The introduction should be no more than 150 words. Start with a relatable hook that acknowledges the reader's pain. End with a clear statement of what they will learn in the article."

Do not ask the AI to write the entire article at once. It is far more effective to work section by section. This "chunking" method gives you more control and allows you to refine the output at each step. After the AI generates the introduction, you can give it feedback and then ask it to write the first main section of the outline. This iterative conversation between you and the AI is what produces a high-quality draft. If the tone is wrong, tell it. "That's a good start, but make the tone a bit more urgent. Rewrite it to emphasize the financial risk of the problem."

Stage Four: The Human Imperative, Editing for Authenticity

If you stop at Stage Three, you will fail. The internet is already becoming flooded with undifferentiated, robotic AI-generated text. Your competitive advantage, and your ethical responsibility, lies in the fourth stage: rigorous human editing. An AI can create a grammatically correct and logically structured draft, but it cannot inject genuine personality, tell compelling stories, or verify the truth. That is your job.

Your first task as the human editor is to be the Fact-Checker. AI models are notorious for "hallucinating" wherein they confidently state incorrect information. You must assume that every statistic, every name, and every factual claim in the AI's draft is wrong until you have personally verified it from a primary source. Skipping this step is not just lazy; it is dangerous to your brand's credibility.

Your second task is to be the Storyteller. AI deals in patterns and generalities; humans connect with specifics and stories. This is where you weave in your unique perspective. Add a personal anecdote about a time you struggled with the problem you're describing. Include a short, real-world case study from one of your pilot customers. Replace a generic example with a specific, vivid one from your own experience. This is what transforms the content from an information dump into a memorable, persuasive asset.

Finally, you must be the Guardian of the Brand Voice. Read the entire piece out loud. Does it sound like you? Does it reflect your company's personality? Rewrite awkward sentences. Break up long, dense paragraphs. Ensure the rhythm and flow of the language are engaging. The AI provides the clay, but you are the sculptor who shapes it into a work that is uniquely yours. This final 20% of human effort is what creates 80% of the value and builds a genuine connection with your audience.

Stage Five: AI as Your Content Repurposing Engine

Once you have a finished, polished, and human-approved piece of core content, such as a comprehensive blog post, the AI's work is still not done. One of the most powerful and efficient uses of AI in a content workflow is for repurposing. You can take one piece of "pillar" content and use AI to atomize it into dozens of smaller "micro-content" assets for different platforms, dramatically increasing the return on your initial time investment.

Feed your final blog post into an AI and give it a series of simple commands:

"Generate five engaging LinkedIn posts based on this article. Each post should
   highlight a different key takeaway and end with a question to encourage comments."

"Create a 10-tweet thread summarizing the main points of this article. Make the
   first tweet a strong hook and the last tweet a call to action to read the full post."

"Write a 200-word summary of this article to be used in our weekly email
   newsletter. The tone should be casual and personal."

"Turn the main sections of this article into a script for a 3-minute YouTube video.
   The script should be conversational and include suggestions for on-screen visuals.

In less than ten minutes, you have transformed one asset into a full week's worth of promotional content tailored for different channels. This content multiplier effect is a superpower for a lean startup. It allows you to maintain a consistent presence across multiple platforms without having to create new content from scratch for each one.

Beyond Text: Generating Visuals and Audio with AI

While text is often the foundation of a content strategy, AI's capabilities extend to other media. AI image generation tools like Midjourney, DALL-E, or Stable Diffusion can create unique, high-quality images for your blog posts, social media, and advertisements. Instead of relying on generic stock photos, you can generate a custom illustration that perfectly matches the topic of your article. As with text, this requires skillful prompting to get the desired style, composition, and mood, ensuring the visuals are consistent with your brand identity.

The same principle applies to audio. There are now highly realistic AI text-to-speech tools that can turn your finished blog posts into audio articles or even standalone podcast episodes. This caters to an audience that prefers to consume content while commuting or exercising. You can also use AI tools to generate royalty-free background music for your videos or podcasts, adding a layer of professional polish without the cost of a sound engineer.

By integrating these tools into your workflow, you can efficiently produce a rich, multi-format content experience that meets your audience wherever they are and however they prefer to consume information. This holistic approach turns your content operation from a simple blog into a true media engine for your business.

* * *

18

Customer Support Automation

For a new business, customer support can feel like a double-edged sword. On one hand, every question from a user is a gift, a precious, real-time signal about a point of confusion in your product, a gap in your documentation, or an opportunity for improvement. On the other hand, the sheer volume of these questions can quickly become overwhelming, a relentless tide of administrative work that pulls you away from building and growing your business. For decades, founders have faced a difficult trade-off: provide fast, personal support and sacrifice scalability, or scale the business and watch support quality decline. Artificial intelligence has shattered this trade-off.

Modern AI allows you to build a customer support system that is not only more efficient but also faster, more consistent, and more proactive than a purely manual approach could ever be. This is not about replacing humans with unfeeling robots to cut costs. It is about strategically augmenting your human team with tireless AI agents that can handle the vast majority of repetitive, common inquiries, freeing up your valuable human experts to focus on the complex, high-stakes issues where their empathy and problem-solving skills are most needed.

Automating customer support is the process of building a layered, intelligent system that empowers users to find answers themselves, provides instant solutions through AI agents, and seamlessly escalates issues to a human when necessary. It is about creating an experience where a customer gets the right answer, through the right channel, in the fastest possible time. For an AI-based business, mastering this is not just an operational advantage; it's a demonstration of your own product's philosophy, using technology to solve problems with unprecedented speed and intelligence.

The Support Pyramid: A Layered Defense

Effective support automation is not a single tool; it's a tiered strategy. Think of it as a defensive pyramid, with each layer handling a larger volume of inquiries, allowing only the most difficult and unusual issues to reach the top. By building this pyramid, you create a system that scales gracefully, providing instant gratification for the majority of users while ensuring the complex cases get the expert attention they deserve.

At the broad base of the pyramid is your Self-Service Layer. This is the foundation of your entire support strategy. It consists of all the resources a user can access on their own, without interacting with anyone. The primary component of this layer is the comprehensive, well-organized knowledge base we discussed during the on-boarding chapter. This is your single source of truth, a library of clear, concise articles, how-to guides, video tutorials, and answers to every frequently asked question you can imagine. Every dollar you invest in making this knowledge base great will pay you back tenfold in reduced support tickets.

The middle layer of the pyramid is the Automated Support Layer powered by AI. This is where you place your AI chatbots and support agents. These agents are the interactive front door to your knowledge base. Their job is to understand a user's question in natural language and instantly provide the relevant answer from the self-service resources you've created. This layer acts as a powerful filter, intercepting and resolving the vast majority of questions that users would otherwise send to your support email. It provides the 24/7, instant response that modern customers have come to expect.

At the very peak of the pyramid is the Human Support Layer. This is where your expert human team resides. The goal of the first two layers is to protect this layer's time fiercely. By successfully deflecting the common and repetitive questions, the pyramid ensures that when a customer issue finally reaches a human, it is a problem worthy of their attention. These are the complex edge cases, the sensitive billing disputes, or the moments when a frustrated user simply needs the empathetic ear of another person. This layer is small, expensive, and incredibly valuable. Your entire automation strategy is designed to deploy this resource with surgical precision.

Laying the Foundation: The AI-Ready Knowledge Base

Your AI support agent is only as smart as the library you give it to read. Before you can even think about implementing a chatbot, you must ensure the base of your pyramid, your knowledge base, is solid. An AI trained on a sparse, poorly written, or out-of-date set of help articles will be useless. It will consistently fail to find answers and will frustrate users, defeating the entire purpose of automation.

Building an AI-ready knowledge base begins with a commitment to documentation. Every time you answer a question from a pilot user or a new customer, ask yourself: "Should this be an article?" If there's even a small chance another user will have the same question, the answer is yes. This turns every support interaction into a content creation opportunity.

Structure your articles for both human and machine readability. Use clear, descriptive titles that sound like the question a user would actually ask. A title like "How do I change my password?" is far better than a generic title like "Account Settings." Use simple language, short paragraphs, and formatting like headings and bullet points to break up the text. This not only helps a human reader scan the article quickly but also provides clear structural cues for an AI trying to parse the information.

Remember that an AI doesn't just read the text; it looks for connections. You can help it by being consistent with your terminology. If you refer to a feature as the "Project Dashboard" in one article, don't call it the "Main Hub" in another. This consistency helps the AI understand the core concepts of your product. As you build out this library, use a dedicated knowledge base platform like Help Scout, Zendesk Guide, or even a tool like FuseBase. These platforms are designed for this purpose, with features for categorization, search, and, increasingly, direct integration with their own AI tools.

Activating Your AI Agent: The Reactive Support Layer

With a robust knowledge base in place, you are ready to deploy your first AI support agent. This chatbot, embedded in your application or on your website, will act as the tireless front-line soldier of your support operation. Its primary directive is to understand a user's question and find the answer within the knowledge base.

Choosing the right tool is your first step. There is a wide spectrum of options available. Platforms like Intercom or Drift offer sophisticated chatbot solutions that are deeply integrated with their customer messaging platforms. They come with visual editors that allow you to design conversational flows and connect directly to your help center articles. For an even more customizable approach, tools like Voiceflow or Botpress let you build truly bespoke conversational AI agents that can be deployed on multiple channels.

The training process is crucial. You will typically start by pointing the AI tool to your knowledge base URL. The AI will then "ingest" all of your articles, creating its own internal map of the information. But don't stop there. The best systems allow you to supplement this with additional context. You can upload documents containing your internal policies, your pricing details, and even transcripts of past support conversations (after carefully anonymizing them to protect user privacy). This richer dataset gives the AI more context to draw from, increasing its accuracy.

The most important part of this training is teaching the AI when to give up. The most frustrating chatbot experience is one that gets stuck in a loop, endlessly repeating the same unhelpful answer. You must design a graceful Human Handoff Protocol. This is a set of rules that tell the AI when to stop trying and escalate the issue to a person. You should configure your bot with an explicit instruction: "If you are asked the same question twice and cannot find a relevant answer in the knowledge base, or if the user types 'talk to a human,' you must immediately stop and execute the human handoff procedure." This escape hatch is essential for maintaining user trust.

Designing the Handoff: From Bot to Human Seamlessly

A successful handoff is one that is invisible and friction-less for the customer. The cardinal sin of support automation is forcing a user to repeat themselves. When the AI escalates an issue, it must pass the entire context of the conversation to the human agent. The human should be able to see the user's name, their account details, their original question, and the full transcript of their chat with the bot.

This is achieved through integration. When your AI bot triggers the handoff, it should also trigger a workflow in your integration platform. This workflow should automatically create a new support ticket in your help-desk system (e.g., Zendesk, Help Scout). The workflow will populate this new ticket with all the contextual information from the chat.

Imagine a user is chatting with your AI agent. The AI fails to answer their question about a specific invoice. The user types "talk to a human." In the background, your workflow kicks in. It creates a new ticket in Help Scout. The ticket is assigned to your support queue. The ticket's subject is "Chat

Handoff from [User Name]." The body of the ticket contains the full chat transcript. The sidebar of the ticket automatically displays a link to the user's profile in your billing system.

When your human agent logs in, they see this ticket waiting. They can read the entire history in seconds. They don't have to ask, "Who are you?" or "What was your question?". They can start their reply with, "Hi Jane, I see you were asking the bot about your invoice from May. I've pulled it up right here and I can see the issue..." This is a world-class support experience, and it is enabled by a thoughtfully designed automation that bridges the gap between the bot and the human.

Closing the Loop: The AI Improvement Cycle

The job isn't finished when the human agent solves the customer's problem. That is only the halfway point. A world-class support system is a learning system. Every single human-handled ticket represents a failure of your automated layers, and therefore an opportunity to make them smarter. This "closing of the loop" is what separates a static support system from an evolving, intelligent one.

You must create a formal process for analyzing your support tickets and feeding the lessons back into the system. This should be a regular ritual for your team, perhaps on a weekly basis. For each ticket that required human intervention, ask a simple question: "Why did the automation fail?" The answers will generally fall into one of two categories.

The first category is a Knowledge Gap. The user asked a question for which no answer existed in your knowledge base. The solution is simple: write a new help article that answers that question. By consistently doing this, you are using your customers' real-world problems to build an ever-more-comprehensive self-service library. Over time, the number of questions that fall into this category should decrease.

The second category is a Retrieval Gap. The answer did exist in the knowledge base, but the AI agent was unable to find it or understand its relevance. This indicates a problem with the AI's training or the way the information is structured. The solution might be to rephrase the title of the help article to be more explicit. It might involve adding more keywords to the article. Or it might require you to provide specific feedback to the AI model itself, a feature offered by many modern support platforms, where you can link a specific conversation to a specific article and tell the AI, "You should have used this article to answer that question."

This continuous improvement cycle is the engine of support scalability. Every ticket you resolve becomes an investment in preventing future tickets of the same type. You are not just putting out fires; you are installing a better fire prevention system each time. This is how a small team can support a rapidly growing user base without a corresponding explosion in support headcount.

Proactive Support: The Final Frontier

Everything we have discussed so far has been reactive. A user has a problem, they ask a question, and your system responds. The highest level of support automation transcends this model. It aims to solve problems before the user even knows they have them. This is the realm of proactive support and it is powered by workflows that monitor user behavior for signals of frustration or confusion.

You can set up automated triggers based on user actions (or inactions) within your application. The goal is to identify moments where a user is likely to be struggling and to offer help before they have to ask for it. This turns your support from a passive resource into an active, guardian angel for your users.

Consider these examples of proactive support workflows:

The "Stuck in Setup" Trigger: Your system detects that a new user has started your setup wizard but has not completed it after three days. This is a massive red flag for churn. A workflow can automatically send a friendly, low-pressure email: "Hi Alex, just wanted to check in. I see you started getting set up but haven't finished yet. The final step can sometimes be tricky. Here's a link to a 2-minute video that might help. Is there anything I can clarify for you?"

The "Repeat Feature Failure" Trigger: Your analytics show that a user has tried to use a specific feature, for example, exporting a report, three times in a row, and each time it has failed due to an error. Instead of waiting for them to file a bug report, your workflow can proactively create a high-priority support ticket for your team and send an email to the user: "Hi Ben, it looks like you might be running into an issue with our report exporting feature. Our engineering team has been automatically notified and is looking into it. We'll let you know as soon as we have an update."

The "Help Doc Binge" Trigger: A user has visited the same three pages in your knowledge base multiple times in the last hour. This is a clear signal that they are confused about a specific topic and are not finding the answer. A workflow could trigger an in-app chat message: "Hey, it looks like you're digging into our client management features. It can be a complex topic! Would you like to schedule a quick 15-minute call with one of our specialists to walk you through it?"

This proactive approach is the pinnacle of a great customer experience. It shows users that you are paying attention and that you are invested in their success. It solves problems when they are small, before they fester into major frustrations. And, like every other part of this system, it can be almost entirely automated, allowing you to provide this white-glove level of service to every single user, at scale. This is how you transform customer support from a necessary cost center into one of your company's most powerful engines for customer retention and brand loyalty.

CUSTOMER SUPPORT AUTOMATION

* * *

19

Measuring KPIs and Analytics

For the first few weeks or months of your startup's life, you can run the business from your inbox and your intuition. You know every customer by name, you feel every success and every failure personally, and your gut tells you what's working and what isn't. This is a beautiful and necessary phase of company building, but it has a very short shelf life. As your user base grows from ten to one hundred, and from one hundred to one thousand, intuition is no longer a reliable guide. To navigate the complexities of growth, you need a different set of senses. You need data.

This chapter is about building the nervous system of your business, the system that translates the raw, chaotic activity of the marketplace into a clear, understandable set of signals. These signals are your Key Performance Indicators (KPIs), a curated set of metrics that tell you the objective truth about your company's health. They are the instruments on your cockpit dashboard, guiding your decisions with facts, not feelings. Without them, you are flying blind, burning through fuel with no idea if you are gaining altitude or heading for a nosedive.

The world of analytics can seem intimidating, a confusing alphabet soup of acronyms and ratios. The goal is not to track every single metric imaginable.

That is a path to "analysis paralysis," where you are drowning in data but starved for insight. The goal is to be a minimalist, to deliberately choose the few vital signs that are most predictive of your success. For an AI business, this means tracking not only the standard business metrics but also a unique set of indicators related to the performance and cost of your AI engine itself.

The Pirate's Map to Growth: AARRR!

One of the most enduring and useful frameworks for thinking about business metrics was developed by investor and entrepreneur Dave McClure. It's known as "Pirate Metrics" because its acronym, AARRR, sounds like a pirate's growl. It breaks the customer life cycle into five distinct stages, each with its own set of questions and corresponding KPIs. It provides a simple, narrative structure for your analytics, telling a complete story from a user's first encounter with your brand to them becoming a passionate advocate.

The five stages are:
1. Acquisition: How do users find us?
2. Activation: Do users have a great first experience?
3. Retention: Do users come back?
4. Revenue: How do we make money?
5. Referral: Do users tell others?

By tracking a handful of key metrics in each of these categories, you can pinpoint the strengths and weaknesses of your business with remarkable clarity. You can see not just that you have a problem, but where the problem is. Is your website not attracting enough visitors (an Acquisition problem), or are visitors arriving but failing to sign up (an Activation problem)? The AARRR framework gives you a map to diagnose your business and focus your efforts where they will have the most impact.

Acquisition: The Top of the Funnel

The Acquisition stage is concerned with how potential customers discover your business. It is the first touchpoint, the moment a stranger becomes a visitor. Your goal here is to measure the effectiveness of your marketing and outreach channels, as defined in your Go-to-Market strategy (Chapter 11). You need to know which channels are bringing you traffic and, more importantly, which channels are bringing you the right kind of traffic.

The most fundamental Acquisition KPI is Website Traffic. This is the total number of unique visitors arriving at your landing page. You can track this with a free tool like Google Analytics. While it's a simple count, it's the baseline for everything else. No traffic, no business.

But not all traffic is created equal. The Click-Through Rate (CTR) of your marketing campaigns tells you how compelling your message is. If 10,000 people see your ad but only 100 click on it, your CTR is 1%. This metric helps you optimize your ad copy and imagery.

Ultimately, the most important Acquisition metric is your Customer Acquisition Cost (CAC). This is the total amount you spend on sales and marketing in a given period, divided by the number of new customers you acquired in that same period. If you spent $1,000 on LinkedIn ads in a month and got 10 new paying customers, your CAC for that channel is $100. Knowing your CAC is absolutely critical because it allows you to make rational decisions about your marketing spend. If your CAC is higher than the lifetime value of a customer, your business is a leaky bucket, losing money on every new user.

Activation: The Magic Moment

A visitor arriving at your website is a good start, but it's a long way from a successful business. The Activation stage is about measuring how effectively you guide that new visitor to the "aha!" moment we discussed in Chapter 14. It is the measure of your product's first impression. A user is "activated" when they successfully experience the core value that you promised.

A key leading indicator is your Sign-up Rate or Conversion Rate. This is the percentage of visitors who take the desired action on your landing page, usually signing up for a free trial or creating an account. If 1,000 people visit your site and 50 sign up, your conversion rate is 5%. A low conversion rate can indicate a problem with your landing page copy, your value proposition, or your pricing.

Beyond the initial sign up, the true measure is the Activation Rate. This is the percentage of new users who complete a specific, critical action that you have identified as being predictive of long-term retention. For an AI transcription service, this might be "successfully transcribing their first audio file." Tracking this metric tells you how effective your on-boarding flow is.

Another critical Activation metric is Time to Value (TTV). How long does it take, on average, for a new user to get from sign-up to that "aha!" moment? Is it five minutes or five days? The longer the TTV, the more likely a user is to lose interest and churn. Your goal should be to relentlessly shorten this time frame by removing friction from your on-boarding process. Tools like Mixpanel, Amplitude, or Heap are designed specifically for this kind of in-product user behavior analysis.

Retention: The Leaky Bucket Test

Acquiring a new customer is expensive. Keeping an existing one is profitable. The Retention stage is arguably the most important part of the AARRR framework for a subscription business. It measures your ability to deliver ongoing value and keep your customers coming back. Without strong retention, your business is a leaky bucket; you can pour new users in the top, but they will drain out the bottom just as fast.

The inverse of retention is Churn Rate. This is the percentage of your customers who cancel their subscription in a given period. If you start a month with 100 customers and 5 of them cancel, your monthly user churn rate is 5%. High churn is a fatal disease for a startup. It indicates a fundamental mismatch between your product and the market's needs. You must monitor this metric obsessively.

To understand engagement, you will track Daily Active Users (DAU) and Monthly Active Users (MAU). The ratio of DAU to MAU is a powerful indicator of your product's "stickiness." If a high percentage of your monthly users are also logging in every day, it means your service is becoming an integral part of their workflow.

The ultimate measure of a retained customer's worth is Customer Lifetime Value (LTV). This is a prediction of the total revenue your business will earn from an average customer before they churn. There are complex ways to calculate this, but a simple formula for an early-stage startup is: (Average Revenue Per User) / (User Churn Rate). Your LTV is the other side of the CAC coin. The golden rule of a sustainable SaaS business is that your LTV must be at least three times your CAC (LTV > 3x CAC). This ensures that each new customer you acquire generates a healthy profit over their lifetime.

Revenue: The Bottom Line

This stage is the most straightforward. Are you making money? While profitability might be a long-term goal, tracking your core revenue metrics from day one is essential. These metrics are the direct output of your pricing strategy (Chapter 12).

For a subscription business, the North Star revenue metric is Monthly Recurring Revenue (MRR). This is the predictable revenue you can expect to receive every month from all your active subscriptions. It is the lifeblood of your company. You should track not just the total MRR, but its components:

New MRR (from new customers), Expansion MRR (from existing customers upgrading to a higher plan), and Churned MRR (from customers who cancel or downgrade). A healthy business has strong Expansion MRR, indicating that your customers are growing with you.

Another important metric is Average Revenue Per User (ARPU). This is your total MRR divided by your number of customers. Tracking ARPU helps you understand the average "size" of your customer and can inform your efforts to move upmarket or offer more valuable plans. All of these revenue metrics can be tracked automatically using a payment platform like Stripe, which has excellent built-in analytics dashboards.

Referral: The Engine of Virality

The final stage of the funnel is Referral. This is when your existing customers become your marketing channel. A strong referral loop is the holy grail of startup growth, as it creates an organic, self-sustaining engine that drives down your Customer Acquisition Cost.

The most popular way to measure customer happiness and referral potential is the Net Promoter Score (NPS). As discussed in the pilot testing chapter, this simple survey question, "How likely are you to recommend us?" is a powerful leading indicator of word-of-mouth growth. A high NPS suggests your customers are not just satisfied, but are actively promoting your service to their peers.

A more direct measure is the Viral Coefficient. This metric calculates how many new users are generated, on average, by each existing user. If every 100 users you have invites enough of their friends to bring in 20 new users, your viral coefficient is 0.2. A coefficient greater than 1 means your product has achieved true viral growth, where each user brings in more than one additional user, leading to an exponential increase in your user base. While achieving this is rare, tracking your referral rates is key to understanding the potential for organic growth.

The AI Engine Dashboard: Metrics for Your Machine

The AARRR framework provides a comprehensive view of your business's health, but as an AI startup, you have a second, equally important engine to monitor: your AI itself. The performance and cost of your underlying AI models have a direct impact on your customer experience and your unit economics. You need a separate dashboard to track these AI-specific KPIs.

First and foremost is Model Performance and Accuracy. Is your AI doing its job correctly? The specific metric here depends entirely on your service. For a transcription service, it would be the Word Error Rate (WER). For a classification tool, it would be Precision and Recall. The key is to have an objective, quantitative measure of your AI's quality. You need to know if a new change you made to a prompt or a model has improved or degraded the quality of the output.

This leads to a crucial operational metric: the Human-in-the-Loop Rate. What percentage of your AI-generated outputs require manual review or correction by a human before they can be delivered to the customer? If 50% of your outputs need to be fixed manually, your service is not scalable. Your goal should be to systematically drive this number down by improving your AI's accuracy. This metric is a direct measure of your operational leverage.

On the financial side, you must obsessively track your Unit Economics. Specifically, you need to know your Average Cost Per Task. How much does it cost you in API fees to perform the core function of your service one time? If you run a report summarization service, you need to know the average cost of summarizing one report. This is calculated by tracking your API usage with your AI provider (e.g., OpenAI, Anthropic).

Knowing this number allows you to calculate your Gross Margin Per

Customer. If a customer pays you $50 per month and, on average, you spend $10 per month on API calls to service that customer, your gross margin is 80%. A high gross margin is essential for an AI business, as it provides the profit needed to cover all your other costs, like research, development, and marketing. If your API costs are eating up most of your revenue, your business model is not sustainable.

Building Your Command Center

Collecting all this data is useless if it lives in ten different spreadsheets and dashboards. You need to bring your most important KPIs together into a single, centralized "Command Center" dashboard. This is your single source of truth, a place you can check every morning to get a real-time snapshot of your business's health.

You don't need a complex business intelligence platform to start. You can build your first dashboard for free using a tool like Google Data Studio. You can connect it directly to sources like Google Analytics, Google Sheets (where you might manually track some data), and your database.

Your dashboard should be ruthlessly simple. Resist the temptation to display 50 different charts. Focus on the 5-10 KPIs that are most critical to your business right now. For an early-stage startup, these might be: MRR, Churn Rate, CAC, LTV, and your primary Activation metric. This focused view allows you to see what matters most at a glance.

At the center of this dashboard should be your North Star Metric. This is the one single metric that, above all others, best captures the core value you are delivering to your customers. For Facebook, it was "Monthly Active Users." For Airbnb, it was "Nights Booked." For an AI service like ClientFlow AI, it might be "Active Client Portals." Your North Star Metric should be something that, if it were to go up, would be a strong indicator that your entire business, from user satisfaction to revenue, is heading in the right direction. It is the compass that aligns your entire team, giving everyone a single, clear target to aim for.

The Rhythm of Review: Turning Data into Action

Data is a tool for decision-making. The final step in building a data-driven culture is to establish a regular rhythm for reviewing your metrics and turning them into action. This is not something to be checked randomly; it should be a formal part of your company's operating cadence.

Institute a Weekly KPI Review Meeting. This could be a 30-minute meeting every Monday morning with your founding team. The agenda is simple: go through your main dashboard. What went up? What went down? Why do we think that happened? What is the most important thing we can do this week to improve one of these numbers? This simple ritual forces you to confront the objective reality of your business every single week and make concrete plans based on the data.

This process transforms analytics from a passive reporting function into an active, strategic one. It allows you to run your business like a series of scientific experiments. You formulate a hypothesis ("If we change the headline on our landing page, our conversion rate will increase"), you run the experiment, and you measure the results with your KPIs. This cycle of hypothesis, experiment, and measurement is the engine of sustainable growth. It replaces the chaos of guesswork with the clarity of evidence, allowing you to navigate the long and challenging journey of building your business with a clear and accurate map.

* * *

20

Lean Project Management for AI Startups

Your business is no longer an idea. It is a living, breathing entity with customers to serve, workflows to execute, and a growing list of bugs to fix and features to build. In the exhilarating chaos of these early days, your greatest danger is not a single, catastrophic failure, but a slow, creeping death by a thousand unfocused tasks. Without a system to manage your time and energy, you will find yourself constantly pulled in a dozen different directions, reacting to the urgent at the expense of the important, and making little tangible progress on any front. You need a system for turning your ambitious vision into a series of small, manageable, and impactful actions. You need a project management philosophy built for the unique uncertainties of the AI world.

Traditional project management, with its exhaustive upfront planning, detailed Gantt charts, and rigid timelines, is poison for a startup. It is a relic of a world where the problem and the solution were known quantities, and the primary challenge was execution efficiency. That is not your world. You are operating in a state of high uncertainty, where your core product is an experiment, your market is a hypothesis, and your AI models are predictably unpredictable. A rigid plan is a fragile plan. What you need is not a map, but a compass, a system that helps you navigate, adapt, and learn with maximum speed and minimum waste.

This is the essence of Lean Project Management. It is a philosophy borrowed from the manufacturing world and adapted for the chaos of startups, with a single, guiding principle: relentlessly eliminate waste. In this context, "waste" is defined as any activity that does not create value for the customer or contribute to validated learning for the business. Writing code for a feature nobody wants is waste. Spending a week debating a decision that could be tested in an hour is waste. Working on five different things at once and finishing none of them is waste. Lean project management is the operational discipline of focusing your limited resources on the things that truly matter.

The Compass of a Lean Startup: Core Principles

To navigate the fog of uncertainty, you need a set of guiding principles. Lean project management is not a strict set of rules, but a mindset. Internalizing this mindset will allow you to make better decisions, faster, and build a culture of focused execution, even if you are a team of one. These principles are your compass, always pointing you toward value and learning.

The first principle is an unwavering Focus on Customer Value. Every task, every feature, every experiment must be justified by a simple question: "How does this make the customer's life better?" This forces you to think from the outside in. Instead of building a feature because it seems cool or technically interesting, you build it because you have direct evidence from customer feedback that it will solve a real problem. If you cannot draw a straight line from the task you are working on to a tangible customer benefit, you should seriously question whether it is worth doing at all.

The second principle is to work in Small Batches. The human brain, and by extension, the startup, is terrible at estimating large, complex projects. A task like "Build a new reporting dashboard" is a black hole of unknown complexity. A lean approach breaks this down into the smallest possible shippable increments. The first task is not to build the dashboard, but to "Create a button on the main screen that links to a blank page titled 'Reports.'" The next task is "Add a single, hard-coded number to the reports page." By breaking the work into tiny, testable pieces, you dramatically reduce risk. If you discover an approach isn't working, you have only wasted a few hours, not a few weeks. This iterative approach allows you to learn and adjust course in real-time.

The third principle is to Visualize the Workflow. You cannot manage what you cannot see. The most powerful tool in the lean project management arsenal is the Kanban board, a simple visual representation of your work in progress. At its most basic, a Kanban board has three columns: To Do, In Progress, and Done. By writing each task on a card and moving it across these columns, you create a shared, real-time understanding of what is being worked on, what is coming next, and what has been accomplished. This simple act of visualization brings clarity to chaos and exposes bottlenecks that would otherwise remain hidden.

The fourth, and perhaps most counter-intuitive, principle is to Limit Work in Progress (WIP). This is the magic ingredient that makes a Kanban board truly effective. A WIP limit is a rule that you cannot have more than a certain number of tasks in the "In Progress" column at any given time. For a solo founder, that limit might be one. This rule may feel restrictive, but its effect is liberating. It forces you to stop starting and start finishing. It prevents the context-switching penalty that comes from juggling multiple tasks, allowing you to focus your full attention on getting one thing over the finish line. A task that is 90% done provides zero value to a customer. A task that is 100% done is a tangible improvement. Limiting WIP is the discipline of creating that value.

The Lean Toolkit: Your Command and Control Center

These principles are not just abstract ideas; they are meant to be put into practice using a simple but powerful set of tools. You do not need expensive, complicated project management software. You can run a highly effective lean system with tools that are cheap, flexible, and easy to set up. Your command center will consist of three key components: the Kanban board, the backlog, and a prioritization framework.

The Kanban Board: Your Single Source of Truth

The Kanban board is the heart of your operational system. Its purpose is to provide a single, shared view of all the work that is happening. You can create a digital Kanban board using a tool like Trello, Asana, Notion, or ClickUp, many of which have generous free tiers. A physical whiteboard with sticky notes can be just as effective for a small, co-located team.

A good starting point for your board's columns is:

Backlog: This is the deep pool of every idea, feature request, bug report, or experiment

you might ever want to work on. It is deliberately unprioritized. It's the parking lot for

future work.

Prioritized / To Do: This column holds the small handful of tasks that you have decided

are the most important things to work on next. These are the tasks you will pull from for

the current work cycle (e.g., this week).

In Progress: This is the column with the strict WIP limit. It contains only the task (or

tasks) that are actively being worked on right now.

In Review / QA: Once a task is complete, it moves here for testing. This could mean you

are testing it yourself to ensure it works as expected, or you are waiting for feedback from a user.

Done: The finish line. A task only moves here when it is fully "shipped" and delivering
  value to users.

Each task on the board should be a "card" that represents a small, discrete piece of work. A good card has a clear, descriptive title and, crucially, a "definition of done." The definition of done is a simple checklist that must be completed before the card can be moved to the Done column. For a task like "Improve the AI summarization prompt," the definition of done might be: "1. New prompt is written. 2. New prompt has been tested on 10 sample documents. 3. New prompt shows a 15% improvement in accuracy based on our quality metric." This removes all ambiguity and ensures that "done" actually means done.

The Backlog: Taming the Idea Beast

Your backlog will quickly become a sprawling list of hundreds of potential tasks. This is a good thing. It means you have a wealth of ideas for improving your business. The key is to treat the backlog not as a sacred to-do list that must be completed, but as an inventory of options from which you will strategically select.

You need a simple system for capturing ideas and getting them into the backlog from wherever they originate. A customer sends an email with a feature request? It goes into the backlog. You have a sudden insight while in the shower? It goes into the backlog. You discover a bug during your own testing? It goes into the backlog. The goal is to get the idea out of your head and into the system so it can be evaluated later. This frees up your mental bandwidth to focus on the work at hand.

Prioritization: Deciding What Matters Now

The backlog is a list of things you could do. Prioritization is the process of deciding what you should do. This is one of the most high-leverage activities a founder can perform. A disciplined prioritization process ensures you are always working on the most impactful task. This should be a data-driven process, not one based on gut feelings or which idea seems most exciting at the moment.

A simple yet powerful prioritization framework is RICE which stands for Reach, Impact, Confidence, and Effort. For each task in your backlog, you give it a score from 1 to 5 on each of these four factors. 1 being the lowest priority and 5 being the highest priority.

Reach: How many users will this task affect? A bug that affects every single user has a

high Reach score. A niche feature for a handful of power users has a low score.

Impact: How much will this task affect those users? Will it provide massive value or a

minor convenience? Fixing a critical workflow failure has a high Impact score. Changing

the color of a button has a low score.

Confidence: How confident are you in your estimates for Reach and Impact? Is this a

data-backed hypothesis from customer interviews, or is it a pure guess? A high

Confidence score means you have strong evidence.

Effort: How much time and work will this task take to complete? A simple text change is

a low Effort. Building a complex new integration is a high Effort.

You can then use a simple formula (Reach x Impact x Confidence) / Effort to generate a RICE score for each task. The tasks with the highest scores are your top candidates to be moved from the backlog into your "Prioritized /

To Do" column. This framework is not a perfect science, but it provides a rational structure for your decision-making, forcing you to think critically about the trade-offs between value and cost for every single task.

The Cadence of Execution: Rituals for Momentum

A system is only as good as the habits that support it. To bring your lean project management system to life, you need a regular rhythm, a cadence of simple rituals that keep the work moving forward and the learning cycle turning. These "meetings," even if they are just appointments with yourself, provide the structure for focused execution.

The cycle begins with a Weekly Planning Meeting. This is a short, 30-minute session at the start of each week. The agenda is simple: look at your "Prioritized / To Do" column (which you've populated using your RICE scores) and decide which one or two tasks you will commit to completing this week. You then pull those cards into the "In Progress" column. This act of public commitment creates focus for the entire week.

To maintain that focus, you have a Daily Stand-up. This is a 15-minute check-in each morning. If you have a team, you do this together. If you are solo, you do it yourself, perhaps by writing a short update in a dedicated Slack channel. You answer three questions:
1. What did I accomplish yesterday?
2. What will I work on today?
3. Are there any obstacles blocking my progress?

This simple ritual prevents drift. It forces you to confront your progress (or lack thereof) every 24 hours and immediately surfaces any roadblocks so they can be addressed.

At the end of a work cycle (e.g., every two weeks), you hold a Retrospective. This is perhaps the most important ritual of all. It is a meeting dedicated to improving your process itself. You ask three questions: What went well in the last two weeks? What went wrong or caused frustration? What is one thing we can change in our process to be more effective in the next cycle? The retrospective is the "Learn" part of the Build-Measure-Learn loop applied to your own operations. It ensures that your team doesn't just get better at building the product, but gets better at the process of building the product.

Lean Management for AI-Specific Work

This lean framework is particularly well-suited to the unique challenges of building an AI-based business. The inherent uncertainty of working with AI models can be managed effectively when you treat every technical task as a small, contained experiment.

When you are trying to improve your AI's performance, don't create a vague task called "Make the AI better." Instead, create a specific experimental card on your Kanban board: "Test Claude 3 Sonnet vs. GPT-4 Turbo for our summarization task." The "definition of done" for this card would be a data-driven conclusion, complete with metrics on cost, speed, and accuracy for both models. The work is not finished until the learning is documented.

This approach also helps you manage the automation of your own workflows. Look at the manual checklist you created for your MVP. Each one of those manual steps is a candidate for an automation task in your backlog. You can use the RICE framework to prioritize them. The step that is most time-consuming (high Impact) and is easiest to automate with a tool like Zapier (low Effort) would get a high RICE score and become a top priority. This allows you to systematically chip away at your manual workload, using your own project management system to guide the process.

The unpredictability of AI is no longer a source of fear; it is simply a variable that the lean system is designed to handle. If an experiment with a new AI model fails, you have not derailed a six-month project plan. You have simply completed a one-day task, learned that a particular approach doesn't work, and are now free to pull the next prioritized task from the backlog. The system's emphasis on small batches and rapid feedback cycles is a perfect match for the experimental nature of applied AI. It turns the uncertainty from a liability into an opportunity for rapid learning and adaptation. This is how you build a business that is not just efficient, but also resilient and durable, a business that gets stronger in the face of the unknown.

* * *

21

Growth Hacking with AI Tools

The traditional path to business growth is a well-trodden one: build a product, raise a marketing budget, buy some ads, hire a sales team, and hope for the best. It is a path paved with significant capital and long time horizons. For a lean startup, this path is often an inaccessible luxury. You do not have the time or the money to follow the old map. You must find the shortcuts, the clever detours, and the hidden leverage points that allow you to outmaneuver, rather than outspend, your competition. This is the path of the growth hacker.

Growth hacking is not a magic trick or a secret formula. It is a mindset, a disciplined process of rapid, data-driven experimentation across the entire customer journey. It rejects the siloed thinking of traditional marketing and sales, instead viewing the entire business, from the first ad a user sees to the wording on a cancellation button, as a single, interconnected system to be optimized for growth. The growth hacker's toolkit is not a large budget, but a deep curiosity, a knack for analytics, and a relentless focus on the user.

Into this world of clever experimentation, artificial intelligence has arrived like a force multiplier. AI provides the modern growth hacker with a set of previously unimaginable superpowers. It is the ability to personalize outreach to thousands of potential customers at once. It is the ability to run a hundred different ad variations in a single day. It is the ability to predict which users are about to leave and to intervene before they do. It is the ability to have a tireless assistant that can write copy, analyze data, and suggest new growth experiments 24/7. For a lean startup, AI is the great equalizer, allowing a small, agile team to execute a growth strategy with the sophistication and scale of a much larger organization.

The Full-Funnel Mindset: Beyond Acquisition

A common mistake is to equate growth hacking with clever tricks to acquire new users. While getting people in the door is a crucial first step, it is only one piece of the puzzle. True growth comes from optimizing the entire customer lifecycle, as mapped by the "Pirate Metrics" (AARRR) framework. A growth hacker is just as concerned with retaining users as they are with acquiring them, because they understand that a business with a leaky bucket cannot grow, no matter how much water you pour into it.

AI can be applied as a lever at every single stage of this funnel. In the Acquisition phase, AI can help you find and attract the right users with unprecedented precision. But its work doesn't stop there. In the Activation phase, AI can create hyper-personalized on-boarding experiences to ensure new users find value immediately. In Retention, it can identify at-risk users and help you keep them engaged. In Revenue, it can help you optimize your pricing and find upsell opportunities. And in Referral, it can pinpoint your happiest customers and help you turn them into your most effective marketing channel.

Adopting this full-funnel mindset is the first step. You stop asking, "How can I get more users?" and start asking more specific, more powerful questions: "What is the biggest bottleneck in my customer journey right now, and how can I use a targeted AI-powered experiment to fix it?" The answer to that question is where sustainable growth begins.

AI-Powered Acquisition: Precision and Personalization at Scale

Your Go-to-Market strategy provided the initial plan for reaching your first customers. Growth hacking with AI takes those foundational tactics and puts them on steroids, enabling a level of scale and personalization that was previously impossible without a large team.

One of the most powerful techniques is Hyper-Personalization at Scale. In Chapter 11, we discussed the importance of personalized outreach. AI can take this to a new level. Imagine you have identified 1,000 potential B2B customers. Manually researching each one to find a personal hook is a monumental task. An AI agent, however, can be programmed to do this automatically. You can build a workflow that takes a list of LinkedIn profiles, feeds each one to an AI, and uses a prompt like: "Review this LinkedIn profile of a marketing manager. Identify their most recent post or a recent company announcement. Draft a single, compelling opening sentence for a cold email that references this specific activity." This allows you to generate a thousand unique, personalized opening lines in the time it would take a human to write five.

Another powerful acquisition hack is Programmatic SEO (pSEO). The concept is to use structured data and templates to generate hundreds or even thousands of unique landing pages, each targeting a very specific long-tail keyword. For example, a service that provides AI-powered menu optimization for restaurants could create a single page template. It could then use AI to generate unique content for every major city and cuisine type. A workflow could automatically create pages for "AI menu optimization for Italian restaurants in Boston," "AI menu optimization for sushi bars in Chicago," and so on. Each page would feature unique, AI-generated text relevant to that specific niche, along with local testimonials if available. This allows a single startup to capture a massive amount of highly specific, high-intent search traffic without manually writing thousands of pages.

When it comes to paid advertising, AI can act as your tireless media buyer. Platforms like AdCreative.ai can generate hundreds of variations of ad copy and creative images in minutes. You can then feed these into platforms like Facebook or Google Ads. The platforms' own internal AI algorithms will then rapidly test these combinations, automatically shifting your budget toward the best-performing ads. This allows you to A/B test on a massive scale, discovering the most effective messaging and imagery far faster than a human could manage through manual trial and error.

Hacking Activation: The Personalized Path to "Aha!"

Getting a user to sign up is a victory, but a fleeting one. The real battle is won during the Activation phase. If a user does not experience the core value of your product quickly, they will churn. AI allows you to move beyond a one-size-fits-all on-boarding flow and create a dynamic, personalized journey for every single user.

The personalization can start on your website itself. Tools like Mutiny or Intellimize use AI to dynamically change the content of your landing page based on the visitor's data, such as their industry, location, or the ad they clicked on. A visitor from a law firm might see a headline that talks about "summarizing legal documents," while a visitor from a marketing agency sees one that talks about "generating client reports." This immediate relevance can dramatically increase your sign-up conversion rate.

Once a user has signed up, the on-boarding flow can be tailored in real-time. By asking a simple question during sign-up ("What is your primary goal with our product?"), you can feed that answer into an AI-powered workflow. This workflow can then customize the entire first-run experience. A user who wants to "save time" might be guided first to your most powerful automation feature. A user who wants to "impress clients" might be shown how to apply their brand's logo and colors to their dashboard. This is the difference between giving every new arrival the same generic city map and giving each one a personalized itinerary based on their interests.

Even the content of your on-boarding emails can be dynamically generated. Instead of a single drip sequence, an AI can craft a unique email based on a user's specific actions (or inactions) within the product. If a user has successfully connected their data source but hasn't run their first report, an AI can generate an encouraging email with a specific tip about the reporting feature. This level of personalization makes the user feel seen and supported, dramatically increasing their chances of reaching that critical "aha!" moment.

Hacking Retention: Predicting and Preventing Churn

A high churn rate is the silent killer of subscription businesses. The traditional approach to churn is reactive: a customer cancels, and you send them a survey asking why. A growth hacker's approach is proactive: use data to predict who is likely to churn and intervene before they hit the cancel button. AI makes this predictive capability accessible to everyone.

You can feed your user analytics data, login frequency, key feature usage, number of support tickets filed, time spent in the app, into a simple AI model. Over time, the model can learn to identify the patterns of behavior that typically precede a cancellation. These are your "churn signals." A user whose login frequency has dropped by 50% in the last month, for example, is a high-risk user.

Once the AI identifies a user at risk of churning, it can automatically trigger a proactive intervention workflow. This is not a generic, "We miss you!" email. It is a targeted, helpful outreach designed to re-engage the user and address their specific problem. The workflow might trigger a personal email from the founder offering a 15-minute feedback call. It could automatically apply a small discount to their next bill. It could send them a link to a new video tutorial for a feature they seem to be struggling with. The key is to test different interventions and measure which ones are most effective at "saving" at-risk users.

AI can also be used to increase retention by driving deeper product adoption. By analyzing a user's current behavior, an AI can intelligently recommend other features they might find valuable. Imagine an in-app notification system powered by AI. Instead of showing every user the same "Did you know?" tip, the AI could generate a personalized recommendation. A user who frequently uses your transcription service might see a message that says, "We noticed you transcribe a lot of meetings. Did you know you can automatically have the transcript sent to your team's Slack channel? Here's how." This helps users discover more value in your product, making it more "sticky" and harder to leave.

Hacking Revenue and Referral: Optimizing the Bottom of the Funnel

The final stages of the funnel, Revenue and Referral, are also ripe for AI-powered growth hacking. These are the levers that directly impact your profitability and your potential for organic, viral growth.

On the revenue front, AI can help you identify upsell and cross-sell opportunities. An AI workflow can monitor a customer's usage against the limits of their current plan. When a user consistently gets close to their monthly report limit or their data storage quota, the AI can trigger a personalized email. The email can congratulate them on their heavy usage and clearly explain the benefits of upgrading to the next tier, framing it as a natural step in their growth journey. This automates a key part of the B2B sales motion, turning your product itself into a salesperson.

For businesses with a high volume of users, AI can even be used to run sophisticated dynamic pricing experiments. While this is an advanced technique, a system could be designed to test small variations in pricing or feature bundling on your website, showing different combinations to different visitor segments and measuring the impact on conversion rate and average revenue per user. This allows you to iterate toward your optimal pricing strategy based on real-world market data.

To amplify referrals, you must first identify your biggest fans. An AI can analyze a combination of signals, high NPS scores, positive support interactions, heavy feature usage, and long retention history, to create a "customer health score." Users with the highest scores are your potential evangelists. Instead of asking every user for a review or a referral, you can use this score to target your requests with precision. A workflow can automatically send a personalized email to these "superfans," asking them if they would be willing to provide a testimonial, participate in a case study, or join your affiliate program. This data-driven approach dramatically increases the quality of your social proof and the effectiveness of your referral engine.

Building Your Growth Stack: The AI-Powered Experimentation Engine

To execute these growth hacks, you need to assemble a "growth stack," a set of interconnected tools that allow you to run experiments, gather data, and automate actions. This stack is the operational embodiment of the growth hacking mindset.

At the base is your Data and Analytics Layer. Tools like Google Analytics, Mixpanel, and Heap are your "senses." They collect the raw behavioral data that tells you what users are actually doing.

Next is your Integration Layer. This is the nervous system, powered by tools like Zapier or Make. This layer allows your other tools to talk to each other, enabling the automated workflows that are the heart of most growth hacks.

The core of the modern stack is the AI and Machine Learning Layer. This includes both the generative AI platforms (like OpenAI, Anthropic, or

Cohere) that create the personalized content and the predictive analytics capabilities that might be built into other tools (like your CRM or customer messaging platform). This is the "brain" that analyzes data and makes intelligent decisions.

Finally, you have your Action Layer. These are the tools that interact directly with the user. It includes your email marketing platform (like ConvertKit), your customer messaging tool (like Intercom), and your website A/B testing framework (like Google Optimize).

A growth hacker's job is to use the integration layer to connect these components into closed-loop systems. Data from the analytics layer is fed into the AI layer for analysis. The AI's insights then trigger a workflow that uses the action layer to run an experiment. The results of that experiment are then measured by the analytics layer, and the cycle begins again. This continuous loop of experimentation, measurement, and optimization is the engine that drives a business from its first user to its first thousand, and beyond. It is the practical application of the scientific method to the art of building a company.

* * *

22

Building and Leading Your AI Team

For a long time, the business has been you. You have been the strategist, the marketer, the salesperson, the AI operator, the customer support agent, and the bookkeeper. Your brain has been the central processing unit for the entire operation. But if your strategies have been successful, you will inevitably arrive at a new and unfamiliar bottleneck: yourself. There are only so many hours in a day, and you have reached their limit. The very success you have worked so hard to achieve has created a new, critical problem, the business has outgrown its founder.

This is the moment you transition from being an entrepreneur to being a leader. It is the point where you must learn to scale not just your technology but also your own impact, by entrusting parts of your creation to others. Hiring your first team members is one of the most significant and nerve-wracking steps in a startup's journey. It means giving up control, spending precious capital, and placing a bet not just on an idea, but on a person. For an AI-native business, this process comes with its own unique set of challenges and opportunities.

You are not hiring for traditional roles defined over decades of corporate history. You are hiring for a new type of work, one that requires a blend of systems thinking, technical curiosity, and a high tolerance for ambiguity. The perfect candidate for your AI startup may not have a perfect resume. They are likely not to be found through traditional recruiting channels. This chapter is your guide to navigating this new talent landscape. It's about how to know when to hire, who to hire, and how to lead a small, agile team that can thrive at the fast-moving frontier of applied artificial intelligence.

The Signals: When to Make Your First Hire

The decision to hire is a major one, fundamentally changing your cost structure and your day-to-day responsibilities. Making your first hire too early can be a catastrophic cash-flow mistake, while hiring too late can lead to founder burnout and stalled growth. The key is to listen for the right signals, the objective indicators that the business is ready for a second person. These signals are not about your ambition; they are about the constraints that are actively holding the business back.

The most common signal is reaching a capacity ceiling. You have more customer demand than you can personally service. You are consistently working unsustainable hours just to keep up with existing orders, and you have no time left to work on the business because you are too busy working in it. Your to-do list for strategic work, like exploring new marketing channels or improving your core AI model, has been gathering dust for months. This is a clear sign that you, as a solo operator, have become the primary bottleneck to growth.

Another clear signal is a persistent skill gap. You have identified a critical business function that is essential for growth but falls far outside your own circle of competence. Perhaps your go-to-market efforts have stalled because you are a product person at heart and have no real expertise in B2B sales. Or perhaps your customer support is suffering because you, the founder, are the only one who can troubleshoot a complex workflow issue. When you can draw a direct line from a lack of a specific skill to a major business problem, it is time to hire that skill.

Finally, look at your financial metrics. Your revenue and, more importantly, your gross margin, must be able to support a salary. A good rule of thumb is to wait until you have enough recurring revenue to comfortably cover the new employee's salary and associated costs for at least six months, even without factoring in the growth they are expected to bring. Hiring on the pure speculation of future revenue is a high-risk gamble. Hiring based on the reality of your current traction is a strategic investment.

Your First Comrades: Defining the Key Roles

When you make your first hire, you are not just hiring a pair of hands; you are hiring a massive portion of your company's future brainpower. For a team of two, your new hire represents 50% of your total workforce. The role they fill must therefore be the one that will have the most immediate and dramatic impact on alleviating your biggest constraint. For most AI-driven service businesses, the first one or two hires will fall into one of three categories.

The most common first hire for a technically-minded founder is a Growth or Sales Lead. This is the person whose sole focus is the top of the AARRR funnel: Acquisition, Activation, Retention, Referral, and Revenue. If you have built a great service but are struggling to find and close deals, this is your most critical need. For a B2B business, this person will be responsible for building lead lists, conducting outreach, performing product demos, and closing contracts. For a B2C business, they will be a growth marketer, focused on running ad campaigns, managing social media, and building community. They are the external-facing part of the company, bringing in the fuel that allows the rest of the business to run.

Conversely, if you are a founder who excels at marketing and sales but finds the operational side of the business to be a struggle, your first hire might be an AI Operator or Operations Lead. This person is the master of your internal engine room. They live and breathe workflows, integrations, and prompt engineering. Their job is to take over the day-to-day execution of the service, to refine and automate the workflows you designed, and to troubleshoot the AI when it produces a wonky result. They are a systems thinker, obsessed with efficiency and reliability. Hiring this person frees you up to focus on what you do best: growing the company.

The third critical role, especially for a service that requires a high degree of trust and interaction, is a Customer Success Lead. This person owns the middle of the funnel: Activation and Retention. Their job is to ensure that every new customer is successfully on-boarded, that they achieve their "aha!" moment quickly, and that they continue to get value from the service over time. They are the human face of your support pyramid, the guardian of your knowledge base, and the champion of the user. In an AI business, where trust is paramount, having a dedicated human focused on the customer experience can be a powerful differentiator.

The Talent Hunt: Where to Find AI Natives

You have defined the role. Now comes the hard part: finding the right person. The challenge is that the titles for these new roles are not yet standardized. You cannot simply post a job for an "AI Workflow Designer" and expect a flood of qualified applicants. You need to look for skills and aptitudes rather than specific job titles on a resume. You are looking for people who are naturally curious, quick learners, and have a demonstrated ability to master new software systems.

One of the best places to look is within the communities of the tools you use. If your business is built on Zapier, Airtable, and Webflow, the official forums and community Slack channels for those platforms are filled with passionate power users. These are people who are already experts in the building blocks of your business. They may be working as freelancers or consultants, and the opportunity to join a startup and apply their skills in a focused way can be very appealing.

Don't underestimate the power of your own network. Announce that you are hiring on your personal LinkedIn profile. Be specific about the problem you are solving and the kind of person you are looking for. Frame it as an opportunity to get in on the ground floor of a fast-moving AI company. The best candidates often come from referrals from people who already know and trust you.

When you write your job description, focus on the outcomes not just the responsibilities. Instead of saying, "Responsibility: Manage our CRM," say, "Outcome: Build and maintain a system that ensures no qualified lead ever gets dropped." Instead of, "Responsibility: Write content," say, "Outcome: Grow our organic search traffic by 50% in the next six months." This outcome-oriented language attracts ambitious, results-focused people, which are exactly the kind of people you need in a startup.

The Lean Hiring Funnel: Testing for Aptitude

As a lean startup, you cannot afford to make a hiring mistake. A bad hire on a team of three is a disaster. Therefore, your hiring process must be a rigorous filter designed to test for real-world skills, not just the ability to write a good resume or answer interview questions. The resume is the beginning of the conversation, not the end.

The most important component of a lean hiring process is the Paid Practical Test. After an initial screening call to gauge communication skills and general interest, you should give your top candidates a small, well-defined project that is a direct sample of the work they would be doing. Crucially, you must pay them for their time. This shows that you respect their work and allows you to ask for a meaningful amount of effort.

For an AI Operator role, the test might be: "Here is a link to a broken 5-step Make scenario. It is supposed to take a form submission and create a research report. Please fix it and document the changes you made. You have three hours." For a Growth Lead role, it might be: "Here is the landing page for our new feature. Please write a 3-email sequence to announce it to our existing users. Draft two different LinkedIn posts about it."

The results of this practical test will tell you more than a dozen interviews ever could. Did they communicate clearly throughout the process? Did they ask smart questions when they got stuck? Was their final work product high quality? And most importantly, did they seem to enjoy the work? The person who is genuinely energized by the practical test is often the right person for the job.

During your interviews, you should screen for adaptability. The AI landscape is incredibly volatile; the hot new model today might be old news in six months. You need people who are masters of learning, not masters of a specific tool. Ask behavioral questions designed to probe this skill. "Tell me about a time you had to become an expert in something you knew nothing about. What was your process?" or "Describe a project that failed. What did you learn from it?". You are looking for a history of curiosity, resilience, and a growth mindset.

Leading the Team: A Culture of Autonomy and Experimentation

Once you have your first team members on board, your role as a founder fundamentally changes. You are no longer the primary "doer." You are now the primary "enabler." Your job is to create an environment where your smart, talented team can do their best work. This requires a leadership style that is radically different from the traditional command-and-control model.

The foundation of this leadership style is empowerment through clear goals. You should not be telling your team how to do their jobs. You should be telling them what success looks like. A framework like Objectives and Key Results (OKRs) is perfect for this. You set a high-level, ambitious Objective (e.g., "Achieve a world-class customer on-boarding experience"). Then, you jointly define a few measurable Key Results that indicate progress toward that objective (e.g., "Increase user activation rate from 40% to 60%," "Reduce Time to Value from 3 days to 1 day," "Achieve a Net Promoter Score of 50 from new users").

With these clear goals in place, you must then give your team the autonomy to figure out how to achieve them. Your Growth Lead doesn't need you to approve every piece of ad copy. Your AI Operator doesn't need you to review every change to a workflow. Your role is to provide the strategic context, remove roadblocks, and act as a sounding board, not to micromanage their tactics. This level of trust is essential for moving quickly.

You must also actively cultivate a culture of psychological safety where experimentation is encouraged and failure is treated as a learning opportunity. If a team member runs a marketing experiment that doesn't work, the correct response is not "Why did you waste that money?" The correct response is "That's an interesting result! What did we learn from this that will inform our next experiment?" When people are not afraid to fail, they are not afraid to take the bold risks that can lead to breakthrough growth.

On-boarding Your Own Team with AI

One of the best ways to build a strong, efficient team culture is to use your own methods on yourself. Apply the same principles of customer on-boarding to your new employee on-boarding. The goal is the same: to get the new hire to their own "aha!" moment, the moment they feel confident and productive, as quickly as possible.

Before your new hire's first day, build them their own On-boarding Portal using a tool like FuseBase or Notion. This portal should be their single source of truth for their first few weeks. It should contain a welcome message from you, a checklist of their on-boarding tasks, links to all the key software tools they'll need, and, most importantly, access to your company's internal knowledge base.

This Internal Knowledge Base is your company's external brain. It is where you document everything: your core business strategy, your detailed customer personas, your brand voice guidelines, and step-by-step documentation for all your key operational workflows. The process of writing this down forces you to clarify your own thinking and creates an invaluable resource that allows new hires to self-serve their questions.

To take this a step further, you can deploy an Internal AI Assistant trained exclusively on this knowledge base. This AI agent can act as a 24/7 on-boarding buddy for your new hire. Instead of interrupting you to ask, "What's our vacation policy?" or "Where do I find the login for our analytics dashboard?", they can simply ask the internal bot. The bot can instantly retrieve the answer from your documented processes. This not only makes your new hire more self-sufficient but also demonstrates the power of the very technology your company is built on.

As your team grows from one to three, and from three to ten, these systems of goal-setting, communication, and knowledge management will be what allows you to scale without chaos. They create a culture of clarity, autonomy, and continuous improvement. Your role as a leader is to be the architect of this culture, to build the scaffolding that enables your team to build the business, and to transition from being the star player to being the coach of a winning team.

* * *

23

Fundraising and Partnerships in AI Business

You have hired your first team members. The business is no longer a solo performance; it's the beginning of an orchestra. With this new capacity comes a new set of challenges and a new, much higher ceiling for your ambitions. You have a validated product, a growing customer base, and a team ready to execute. The machine is built; the question now is how you will fuel it for the journey ahead. Growth requires resources, either the capital to invest in marketing, sales, and product development, or the leverage that comes from strategic alliances.

This brings you to a critical inflection point, a strategic choice that will define the trajectory and culture of your company for years to come. Do you continue on the path of self-sufficiency, funding your growth organically from the revenue you generate? Or do you step onto the high-speed train of external funding, trading a piece of your company for the capital to accelerate your vision? Alongside this financial decision lies a parallel path to growth: the strategic use of partnerships to expand your reach and capabilities without diluting your ownership.

This chapter is about these two powerful levers of growth: fundraising and partnerships. They are not mutually exclusive, but they represent different philosophies and come with different trade-offs. We will dissect the realities of bootstrapping versus venture capital, explore what it takes to secure funding in the competitive AI landscape, and lay out a framework for building alliances that can amplify your growth far beyond what you could achieve alone. This is not about choosing the "right" path; it's about choosing the path that is right for the specific business you want to build.

The Fork in the Road: To Raise or To Bootstrap?

Before you write a single slide of a pitch deck or draft a single partnership proposal, you must answer a fundamental question about your own ambition. What kind of company are you building? Is it a profitable, sustainable business that provides you with freedom and control? Or is it a high-growth rocket ship designed for market domination, with the ultimate goal of a massive exit or an initial public offering (IPO)? The answer to this question will point you toward one of two paths: bootstrapping or venture funding.

The path of the bootstrapper is the path of self-reliance. You fund the business's growth entirely from its own revenue. Your spending is constrained by your sales. This is the ultimate "lean" approach. The primary and most cherished benefit of bootstrapping is that you retain 100% ownership and control of your company. You answer to no one but your customers and your own conscience. You can grow at a pace that feels comfortable, prioritize profitability from day one, and build the exact product and culture you want without outside influence. You are free to build a great business, not just a sellable asset. The trade-off, of course, is speed. Growth is often slower and more methodical, as you can only invest what you earn.

The venture-backed path is a deliberate decision to trade equity for speed. By taking on venture capital (VC), you are selling a portion of your company to investors in exchange for a significant injection of cash. This capital allows you to hire a larger team, spend aggressively on marketing, and build out your product much faster than a bootstrapped competitor could. Along with the money, good investors bring a valuable network of contacts, deep industry expertise, and experience in scaling companies. However, this fuel comes with a heavy set of expectations. You are no longer just building a business; you are managing a financial asset for your investors. They are expecting a massive return on their investment, typically a 10x or greater return within a 5-10 year time frame. This creates immense pressure to grow at all costs, often prioritizing top-line revenue growth over short-term profitability. The company's trajectory is set: go big or go home.

Neither path is inherently superior. A bootstrapped business that grows steadily to $5 million in annual profit can be a phenomenal success for its founders. A venture-backed company that becomes a market leader and exits for a billion dollars is also a phenomenal success. The critical error is to try to walk both paths at once or to take venture capital without fully understanding the implicit contract you are signing. If your goal is to build a lifestyle business, do not take VC money. If your goal is to build the next industry-defining giant, bootstrapping may be too slow.

Navigating the Fundraising Gauntlet

Should you decide that the venture path aligns with your ambitions, you must prepare for one of the most demanding and time-consuming processes a founder can undertake. Fundraising is a full-time job. It requires a thick skin, a compelling story, and, most importantly, evidence of traction. Investors do not fund ideas; they fund businesses that are already showing signs of life.

The first question is always: is it time to raise? The answer lies in your metrics. You are ready to raise your first round of funding, often called a "seed" round, when you have moved beyond your MVP and have clear evidence of Product-Market Fit. This means you have a cohort of happy, paying customers. You have a low churn rate. You can show a positive trend in your Monthly Recurring Revenue (MRR). You have a clear understanding of your Customer Acquisition Cost (CAC) and a plausible case for a high Customer Lifetime Value (LTV). You must also have a credible answer to the question, "What will you do with the money?" You need a specific, data-informed plan for how you will deploy the capital to scale your growth engine, for example, "We will use this $1 million to hire three salespeople and expand our marketing spend, which we project will allow us to acquire 500 new customers over the next 18 months."

The fundraising world has its own cast of characters. Your first outside capital will likely come from Angel Investors. These are wealthy individuals, often successful former entrepreneurs themselves, who invest their own money in early-stage startups. They tend to make smaller investments, write checks faster, and are often more willing to bet on a promising team and an early product. Venture Capital (VC) firms on the other hand, are professional investment funds that invest other people's money. They make larger investments, have a more formal and rigorous due diligence process, and often take a board seat, giving them a direct say in the company's governance.

To approach these investors, you need a pitch deck. This is a concise, 10-15 slide presentation that tells the story of your business. A compelling deck does not just list features. It crafts a narrative that covers:

The Problem: A clear and painful problem experienced by a large market.

The Solution: A simple explanation of your product and why it is a uniquely effective
solution.

The Market Size: Evidence that you are tackling a large and growing market (your Total
Addressable Market, or TAM).

The Product: A live demo or screenshots that prove your product is real and works.

Traction: Your key metrics (MRR, user growth, retention). This is often the most

important slide.

The Team: Why you and your team are uniquely qualified to solve this problem.

The Business Model: Your pricing, CAC, and LTV.

The Ask: How much money you are raising and what you will use it for?

For an AI startup, investors will perform a specific kind of due diligence. They will look past the hype and scrutinize the core of your technology. They will want to know: What is your technical moat? Are you just a "thin wrapper" around a public API like GPT-4, or have you built something genuinely defensible? A moat could be a proprietary dataset you've collected, a unique workflow you've perfected, deep integrations into a specific industry's software ecosystem, or a strong brand built on trust. They will also dissect your unit economics. They'll want to see that you have a firm grasp on your API costs per customer and that your pricing provides a healthy gross margin. Be prepared to answer tough questions about how you handle data privacy and security, as this is a major liability risk for any AI company.

Growth Through Alliances: The Power of Partnerships

Whether you choose to raise capital or not, partnerships offer a powerful, non-dilutive path to growth. A strategic partnership is a formal relationship between your company and another organization that creates mutual value. It can provide you with access to customers, technology, or credibility that would take you years to build on your own. For a small AI startup, partnering with a larger, more established player can be a game-changing move. There are three primary types of partnerships to consider.

Channel Partnerships are all about distribution. You find a larger company that already serves your Ideal Customer Profile and create an arrangement for them to sell or promote your product to their existing customer base. This is a massive shortcut to market access. For example, if your AI service helps e-commerce stores optimize their product descriptions, a channel partnership with a major e-commerce platform like Shopify or BigCommerce could be transformative. Their app store could become your primary acquisition channel, bringing you thousands of qualified leads. The trade-off is that you will typically have to share a percentage of your revenue with the channel partner, but it is often a price well worth paying for instant scale.

Technology Partnerships, also known as integration partnerships, are about making your product work better with the other tools your customers already use. By building a deep, seamless integration between your AI service and another key piece of software, you make both products more valuable and "stickier" for the customer. If your meeting summarizer has a flawless integration with Microsoft Teams, a company that runs on the Microsoft ecosystem is far more likely to choose your solution over a competitor's. These integrations create a powerful defensive moat. The more your product is woven into your customer's core workflow, the harder it is for them to switch to a competitor.

Co-marketing Partnerships are simpler, lower-commitment alliances with non-competing companies that serve a similar audience. You can pool your marketing resources to expand your collective reach. This could involve co-hosting a webinar, writing guest posts for each other's blogs, or running a joint social media campaign. For example, an AI tool for financial advisors could partner with a compliance software company to host a webinar on "The Future of AI and Regulation in Wealth Management." Both companies get exposure to the other's audience for a fraction of the cost of traditional advertising.

Forging the Alliance: How to Secure a Partnership

Initiating and closing a partnership is a process that closely mirrors B2B sales. It requires research, a compelling value proposition, and a clear understanding of the other party's motivations. You cannot simply email a large company and ask, "Will you be my partner?". You must approach them with a well-reasoned business case that clearly answers the question: "What's in it for you?"

Start by identifying potential partners who have a strategic incentive to work with you. A large, incumbent software company might be feeling pressure from more nimble, AI-native competitors. They may be slow to innovate internally. This is your opening. Your small, agile AI startup can be the solution to their problem. You can provide them with the cutting-edge AI capability their customers are asking for, much faster and cheaper than they could build it themselves.

When you reach out, frame the partnership entirely in terms of their goals. How will working with you help them reduce their own customer churn? How will it help them win new deals against their competitors? How can it create a new, high-margin revenue stream for them? Your pitch should not be about your needs; it should be about solving their problems.

For example, when approaching Shopify, you wouldn't say, "We need you to help us get customers." You would say, "We have developed an AI tool that has been shown to increase conversion rates for Shopify merchants by an average of 15%. By integrating our technology into your platform, you can offer a powerful new value proposition to your merchants, increasing their success and your platform's stickiness."

In these negotiations, your AI-native status is your greatest asset. Large companies are often slow-moving and risk-averse. You are fast, focused, and on the cutting edge. You can run experiments and ship features in a week that would take them a year of internal committee meetings to approve. This speed is incredibly valuable. Position yourself as the expert, the agile innovation partner who can help them navigate the complex and fast-changing world of AI.

Building a business is about creating leverage. You can create financial leverage by raising capital, allowing you to do more than your revenue alone would permit. You can create distribution leverage through channel partnerships, reaching more customers than your own marketing could. And you can create product leverage through technology partnerships, building a solution that is more valuable than the sum of its parts. Your job as a founder is to look at these levers and decide which ones to pull, and when, to propel your business forward on its journey from a promising startup to an enduring, market-leading company.

* * *

24

Scaling Operations and Systemizing Success

There is a powerful and dangerous paradox at the heart of every successful startup. The very things that made you successful in the beginning your direct, hands-on involvement in every sale, your personal touch on every customer interaction, your intuitive grasp of every moving part, will eventually become the very things that prevent you from growing. Your business has been powered by your heroic effort. Now, that effort has become the bottleneck. The systems that live inside your head must be extracted, documented, and automated. To scale your business, you must first scale yourself out of the critical path.

This chapter is about a fundamental shift in your role: from the primary doer to the primary designer of systems. It's about moving from ad-hoc processes that work for ten customers to robust, repeatable systems that can work for ten thousand. Scaling is not simply about doing more of the same; it's about building a machine that can do the work without your constant intervention. This means systemizing your workflows, your knowledge, your customer interactions, and even your team's operations. It is the process of deliberately making yourself redundant, so you can finally focus on the one job that only a founder can do: steering the ship, not rowing it.

The journey from a founder-led operation to a systems-driven business is the transition from a startup to a company. It's where you build the operational scaffolding that will support the weight of your future growth. This is not about adding bureaucracy; it's about creating clarity and leverage. It's about building a business that can run, and thrive, even when you take a week off.

From Tribal Knowledge to a Centralized Brain

In the early days, your company's most valuable asset is the knowledge stored in the brains of the founding team. You know the history of every feature, the rationale behind every pivot, and the quirks of every customer. This "tribal knowledge" is a powerful asset for speed and agility, but it is a catastrophic liability for scale. If the answer to a question always begins with "Ask the founder," your business cannot grow beyond the founder's availability. You must build a centralized, external brain for your company.

This external brain is your internal knowledge base, a concept we introduced for on-boarding new hires. At the scaling stage, however, it evolves from a simple welcome packet into the canonical source of truth for the entire company. It is the single place where every process, decision, and piece of critical information is documented. The rule becomes: if it's not in the knowledge base, it doesn't exist. This discipline is the foundation of scalable operations.

Your first task is to document your Standard Operating Procedures (SOPs). An SOP is a detailed, step-by-step checklist for any recurring task in your business. This is not high-level strategy; this is a granular, "click here, then do that" instruction manual. You should have an SOP for everything: how to process a refund, how to onboard a new B2B client, how to publish a blog post, how to handle a data deletion request. The process of writing these SOPs forces you to clarify and standardize your own workflows. Once written, they become invaluable assets for delegating tasks with confidence, ensuring consistency and quality regardless of who performs the action.

Beyond processes, you must document your Decision Logs. When you make a significant strategic choice, like changing your pricing, selecting a key technology vendor, or discontinuing a feature, create a short document that explains the context, the options considered, and the rationale for the final decision. This simple habit is incredibly powerful. It prevents the team from endlessly re-litigating old debates and provides crucial context for future employees who will wonder why the company operates the way it does.

Finally, your company brain must contain a clear map of your System Architecture. This is a document that outlines your entire tech stack. What tools do you use? What is each tool's purpose? How are they connected via APIs and webhooks? Who on the team is the designated "owner" responsible for managing that tool? This map is essential for troubleshooting problems and for planning future integrations. As your stack becomes more complex, this document becomes your operational schematic. Tools like Notion, Confluence, or a self-hosted FuseBase portal are excellent platforms for building this living, breathing company wiki.

Graduating Your Workflows: From MVP Scripts to Robust Automations

The workflows you built in the early stages were designed for speed and learning. They were likely simple, linear automations, connecting a few tools to solve the core problem. As you scale, these MVP-level scripts must graduate into robust, resilient, and fully autonomous systems. This means deliberately engineering them to handle the messiness of the real world, failure, bad data, and unpredictable volume.

The first step is to build in sophisticated Error Handling and Resilience. Your MVP workflow probably followed a "happy path" and simply stopped if something went wrong. A scalable workflow anticipates failure. For every step in your automation (e.g., in a Zapier or Make scenario), you must ask, "What happens if this API call fails?" Instead of the workflow just halting, a professional-grade automation will trigger a specific error-handling sub-routine.

For example, if your AI agent fails to process an uploaded file, the workflow shouldn't just die. It should automatically move the problematic file to a "Manual Review" folder, update the task status in your project manager to "Failed," and send an alert to a specific Slack channel with a link to the file and the error message. This transforms a silent failure into a managed, actionable event. You are building an immune system for your operations.

Next, you must mature your approach to AI Interactions. In the early days, you might have been manually tweaking prompts for individual customers. At scale, this is impossible. You need to systematize your prompt engineering. This means creating a centralized, version-controlled library of your core prompts. When you find a better way to phrase a prompt, you update it in this central library, and all subsequent workflows automatically use the new version. For high-volume, mission-critical tasks, you might even consider graduating from general-purpose models to a fine-tuned custom model. Fine-tuning involves taking a base model and further training it on your own curated dataset of high-quality examples. This can result in an AI that is more accurate, more reliable, and often cheaper to run for your specific use case.

Finally, you must start Monitoring the Performance of your internal systems, not just your public-facing product. Your integration platform's analytics dashboard is a goldmine of operational data. How many times did a specific workflow run this week? What was its success rate? What is the average execution time? By monitoring these metrics, you can identify bottlenecks in your own assembly line. If a particular workflow is slow or has a high failure rate, it becomes a top priority for optimization. You are applying the principles of KPI measurement to your own operational efficiency.

Systemizing the Customer Journey

Your early customers received an incredible amount of personal attention. As you scale, you cannot personally guide every user, but you can use systems to create an experience that feels personal and attentive. This means automating the relationship-building aspects of the customer journey, turning your best practices into repeatable, trigger-based workflows.

The first system to build is an Automated Customer Health Monitoring dashboard. This is a simple but powerful concept. In your CRM or even a sophisticated Airtable base, you can create a "health score" for each customer. This score is a calculated number based on a few key engagement metrics: the date of their last login, their usage of core features, the number of support tickets they've filed, and their payment status. You can create a simple formula that flags customers as "Healthy" (green), "At-Risk" (yellow), or "Critical" (red).

These health scores then become the triggers for Automated, Proactive Communication. You can design email or in-app messaging sequences that are tailored to each segment. A "yellow" at-risk customer might automatically receive a friendly check-in email offering help or a link to a relevant tutorial. A "green" healthy customer, on the other hand, might receive an invitation to your affiliate program or a request for a testimonial. This allows you to provide targeted, relevant outreach to every single customer at scale, something that would be impossible to do manually.

You also need to systematize your Feedback Collection and Analysis. Instead of relying on ad-hoc interviews, you can automate the process. Set up automated surveys to be sent at key moments in the customer lifecycle, for example, 30 days after sign-up or immediately after they use a major new feature. You can then pipe all the open-ended feedback from these surveys into an AI tool for analysis. An AI can perform sentiment analysis, identify the most common keywords, and automatically categorize the feedback into buckets like "Feature Request," "Usability Issue," or "Pricing Feedback." This gives you a real-time, quantitative view of customer sentiment and allows you to spot trends and problems much earlier.

Dashboards as Your Scaled Command Center

The KPI dashboard you built for yourself in Chapter 19 was your personal guidance system. As you scale and build a team, the role of the dashboard evolves. It becomes the company's shared instrument panel, the tool that ensures everyone, from the growth lead to the AI operator, is looking at the same objective reality and rowing in the same direction.

To achieve this, you need to move from a single dashboard to Role-Based Dashboards. Your Growth Lead needs a dashboard that lives and breathes the AARRR funnel: website traffic, conversion rates, CAC, and trial signups. Your Operations Lead, however, needs a dashboard that tracks AI-specific metrics: average cost per task, workflow success rates, and the human-in-the-loop correction rate. Your Customer Success Lead needs to see activation rates, churn rates, and customer health scores. By creating these tailored views, you provide each team member with the specific data they need to make informed decisions within their domain.

The next step is to Automate Reporting. No one should have to manually pull numbers and create reports each week. You can set up your analytics or business intelligence tool to automatically generate and distribute key reports via email or Slack. Every Monday morning, a summary of the previous week's sales and MRR growth can be posted to the general company Slack channel. A daily summary of critical support tickets can be sent directly to the product team. This practice makes data an ambient, ever-present part of the company culture. It removes data from the realm of special occasions and integrates it into the daily rhythm of work.

This systemized approach to data ensures that as the team grows, alignment is maintained through shared facts, not top-down directives. It allows for decentralized decision-making, as a team member can independently see a problem in their dashboard, formulate a hypothesis to fix it, and run an experiment, all without needing a formal meeting to get permission.

The Human Element of Scale: Systemizing Team Operations

Scaling a company is ultimately about scaling a group of people. The systems you build are not just for your technology; they are for your team's collaboration and execution. The goal is to create an operating system for your company that enables high performance and minimizes friction as you grow.

The key to this is to practice Delegation via Systems, Not Instructions. When you delegate a task, you shouldn't just explain it verbally. You should point the team member to the relevant SOP in your internal knowledge base. Their job is not just to follow the SOP but to own it. If they find a better way to do the task, their responsibility is to update the SOP for everyone else. This creates a culture of continuous improvement and empowerment. The system, not the founder, becomes the manager of the process.

As your team grows, especially if it is remote, you must deliberately build an Asynchronous-First Communication Culture. A reliance on synchronous meetings is a major scaling bottleneck. An "async-first" culture assumes that communication should happen in writing or via recorded video messages (using tools like Loom) by default. A meeting is treated as a last resort, reserved only for complex brainstorming or sensitive personnel issues. This culture, supported by tools like Slack for quick updates and your project management board for detailed task-level communication, allows the team to stay aligned and productive without the constant interruption and scheduling nightmare of back-to-back calls.

Ultimately, the test of a successfully scaled operation is simple: can the business function effectively without you for two weeks? If you can go on vacation and return to find that customers have been served, revenue has been generated, problems have been solved, and the team has made progress on key initiatives, you have succeeded. You have built a resilient, systems-driven company, not just a job for yourself. You have built a machine that is bigger than any one person, ready to tackle the next order of magnitude in its growth.

* * *

25

Preparing for the Future of AI in Business

You have reached the final chapter, but you have not reached the end of the journey. In fact, the journey has just begun. The preceding chapters have guided you through a structured process, from the spark of an idea to the construction of a scaled, systematized business. You have built a machine designed to operate in the world of today. This final chapter is about ensuring that the machine is not rendered obsolete by the world of tomorrow. The ground beneath the feet of any AI-based business is not solid; it is a set of constantly shifting tectonic plates. The models, the platforms, and the very definition of what is possible are evolving at a breathtaking, almost dizzying, pace.

Preparing for the future of AI is not about gazing into a crystal ball and making perfect predictions. It is about building a business that is structurally designed for adaptation. The specific tools you have chosen, the workflows you have perfected, and the AI models you rely on are all temporary. Your long-term success will not be determined by your mastery of today's technology, but by your organization's ability to learn, unlearn, and rapidly adopt the technology of tomorrow. This is the final and most critical system to build: an engine for continuous evolution. It's about cultivating a mindset and a culture that sees the relentless pace of change not as a threat, but as an endless source of new opportunities.

The Accelerating Curve of Progress

The history of technological adoption has followed predictable curves, but the slope of the AI curve is unprecedentedly steep. What was considered a state-of-the-art capability eighteen months ago is now a standard, commoditized feature. The leap from one generation of large language models to the next represents a quantum jump in power and reasoning ability. This relentless acceleration means that any business plan tied too tightly to the specific capabilities or limitations of a single model is inherently fragile.

This reality should not be a cause for anxiety, but for a strategic shift in focus. You must accept that you are not in the business of selling a specific AI model's output; you are in the business of solving a specific customer problem. The AI is simply the tool you use to do it. As better tools become available, you must be ready to pick them up. This requires a commitment to what could be called "technological agility", the organizational capacity to evaluate, test, and integrate new AI advancements into your existing workflows with minimal friction.

Your team's most valuable skill is not proficiency in using Gemini, ChatGPT, Claude, or any other specific named model. It is their proficiency in the process of prompt engineering, workflow design, and critical evaluation of AI outputs. These meta-skills are transferable. The founder who knows how to coax a great result from one model will quickly learn how to do the same with a new, more powerful one. The future belongs not to the masters of a single tool, but to the masters of the learning process itself. This means dedicating time and resources, even in a lean startup, pure experimentation, to testing new platforms and models not for immediate ROI, but for the strategic advantage that comes from staying on the leading edge of the curve.

From Co-Pilot to Agent: The Rise of Autonomous Systems

One of the most significant shifts on the immediate horizon is the transition from "co-pilot" AI to "agentic" AI. Most of the systems we have discussed in this book are co-pilots; they are powerful assistants that execute a well-defined task under human supervision. You ask the AI to draft a report, and it drafts a report. You ask it to summarize a document, and it summarizes the document. The future belongs to autonomous agents, systems that can take on a high-level goal, break it down into a series of sub-tasks, execute those tasks using various tools, and adapt their approach based on the results, all without direct human intervention.

Think back to the "Insight AI" research assistant workflow we designed. The current co-pilot version required multiple, distinct steps orchestrated by a tool like Make: search the web, extract text, summarize, format, and then wait for human review. An agentic version of this workflow would be far simpler to command. Your instruction would not be a series of steps, but a single goal: "Create a comprehensive research report on the market for boutique consulting firms, focusing on their technology adoption challenges. The report should be 1,500 words, include data from at least five credible sources, and be delivered to the client by 5 p.m. today."

The AI agent would then autonomously figure out the best way to achieve this goal. It would decide which search queries to run, which sources to trust, how to synthesize the information, and how to format the final report. It might even perform its own quality check, comparing its draft to a set of predefined standards, and decide on its own whether human review is necessary.

The implication for your business is the potential for an even greater degree of operational leverage. Processes that are currently semi-automated, requiring a human-in-the-loop for quality control, could become fully autonomous for a large percentage of cases. This could fundamentally alter your cost structure, allowing you to serve more customers at a lower price point or achieve higher margins.

Preparing for this shift means beginning to think of your workflows not as rigid sequences of commands, but as goal-oriented directives. Start experimenting with emerging agentic AI platforms. Give them simple, multi-step tasks and observe how they perform. Your role will slowly shift from being a micro-manager of AI tasks to being a high-level manager of a digital workforce, setting strategic goals and letting your agents figure out the tactical execution.

The World Becomes Multimodal

For the last few years, the world of generative AI has been largely siloed. You used one tool for text, another for images, another for audio, and another for video. This separation is rapidly collapsing. The next generation of frontier models is inherently multimodal, able to understand, process, and generate content across virtually all media types from a single interface. A single prompt could result in a blog post, a set of illustrations for that post, a short video summarizing it, and the background music for that video.

This convergence of capabilities will unlock entirely new categories of AI-powered services. A customer support interaction will no longer be limited to a text-based chat. A user could upload a screen recording of the problem they are facing. The multimodal AI could watch the video, understand the user's issue, and generate a personalized video response that walks them through the exact clicks needed to solve it, complete with a synthesized voiceover.

A marketing service is no longer just about writing copy. A client could provide a single creative brief, and the AI service could deliver an entire campaign: ad copy for five different platforms, a dozen unique image variations for A/B testing, and a 30-second promotional video for social media.

To prepare for this multimodal future, you must begin to think beyond the primary medium of your current service. If you are a text-focused business, start to build your team's literacy in the principles of visual design and audio production. Start experimenting with today's image, audio, and video generation tools, even if they don't have an immediate application in your current workflow. The goal is to build an intuitive understanding of what makes a good visual or a compelling piece of audio. When the truly powerful, integrated multimodal models become widely available, you will have a significant head start on competitors who are still thinking only in terms of text.

Intelligence Commoditizes, Judgment Becomes Key

As the massive, frontier AI models built by companies like Google, OpenAI, and Anthropic become more powerful, they will also become more like a public utility. Access to raw intelligence will be as common and as commoditized as access to electricity or cloud computing. The simple act of being a "thin wrapper" around one of these public APIs will cease to be a viable long-term business model. If your service is nothing more than a prettier interface for ChatGPT, your business has no defensive moat.

Your competitive advantage will not come from the AI model itself, but from everything you build around it. It will come from your deep, proprietary understanding of a specific customer's problem. It will come from the unique, efficient workflow you have designed to solve that problem. It will come from the trust and brand loyalty you have built through exceptional customer experience. It will come from the proprietary data you have ethically collected and used to fine-tune a model for your specific niche. The value shifts from the raw intelligence to the applied judgment in how that intelligence is deployed.

This trend also points to the growing importance of smaller, specialized AI models. While the frontier models are jacks-of-all-trades, a new ecosystem of powerful open-source models is emerging. These smaller models can be fine-tuned to become world-class experts at a single, narrow task. For a high-volume, repetitive process, it may become much faster, cheaper, and more secure to run your own fine-tuned version of an open-source model rather than sending every request to a large, general-purpose API.

To prepare for this future, it is wise to avoid getting locked into a single AI provider. As you build your systems, think in terms of an "AI abstraction layer." Design your workflows in a way that makes it relatively easy to swap out one AI provider for another. This flexibility will allow you to take advantage of price drops, performance improvements, and new capabilities from across the entire market, rather than being beholden to the roadmap of a single mega-corporation. Your business should be AI-agnostic, always choosing the best engine for the specific job at hand.

The Evolving Team: New Roles for a New Reality

The nature of work in an AI-native company is a moving target. The key roles you hired for in Chapter 22, the AI Operator, the Growth Lead, are themselves just the first iteration. As AI agents become more autonomous and the technology becomes more deeply embedded in every business function, the skills your team needs will continue to evolve.

We will likely see the rise of new, highly specialized roles. An AI Trainer or Prompt Librarian will be responsible for curating the datasets and managing the prompts used to guide the company's AI systems, a sort of digital dog trainer for your workforce of bots. An AI Ethicist or Responsible AI Lead will be tasked with ensuring the company's use of AI is fair, transparent, and compliant with a rapidly changing regulatory landscape. An AI Orchestration Specialist will be an expert in designing and managing the complex interactions between dozens of different AI agents and traditional software applications, the master conductor of the automated orchestra.

The core competency for every employee, from marketing to operations, will be the ability to effectively collaborate with AI. The most valuable team members will be those who can think critically about which tasks are best suited for a human and which are best delegated to an AI. They will be masters of defining goals, providing clear context, and evaluating the output of their digital counterparts.

Your primary role as a leader will be to foster a culture of relentless, continuous learning. The specific software skills a team member has today are far less important than their demonstrated ability to learn and master the next generation of tools. This means you must actively invest in their growth. Create a formal budget for education, giving your team the resources to take online courses, attend conferences, and buy new tools for experimentation. Carve out "innovation time" where team members are encouraged to play with new AI technologies that have no immediate, direct application to their daily work. This investment in your team's adaptability is the single best investment you can make in your company's future resilience.

Navigating the Uncharted Waters of Law and Ethics

The final, and perhaps most unpredictable, frontier is the legal and ethical landscape. The speed of AI development has dramatically outpaced the ability of governments and societal institutions to create clear rules of the road. We are currently in a "wild west" phase, but this will not last. Questions of copyright ownership for AI-generated content, accountability for AI-driven mistakes, and the potential for algorithmic bias are being debated in courtrooms and parliaments around the world.

The regulatory environment of tomorrow will be stricter than it is today. The way you handle data, the transparency you provide about your AI's decision-making processes, and the guardrails you put in place to prevent misuse of your service will all come under increasing scrutiny. A major regulatory shift or a landmark legal ruling could force you to fundamentally change your product or business model overnight.

There is no simple way to prepare for this uncertainty, but the most robust strategy is to build your company on an unwavering foundation of ethical practice and user trust from day one. Do not wait for regulations to force you to be transparent about your data practices; make radical transparency a core part of your brand from the beginning. Do not wait for a lawsuit to force you to think about the potential for your AI to cause harm; build a strong Acceptable Use Policy and proactively monitor for misuse.

By consistently choosing the path that prioritizes your customer's privacy, security, and well-being, even when it is not the most profitable path in the short term, you build a business with a strong moral compass. This is not just a feel-good platitude. In a future where trust is a scarce commodity, the companies that have earned it will be the ones that endure. They will be more resilient to regulatory shocks because they are already operating at a standard higher than what the law requires.

The journey you have taken through this book has equipped you with a set of principles for building a business in this new age: a relentless focus on solving a real customer problem, a lean and iterative approach to development, a commitment to systematic and scalable operations, and a deep understanding of the AI tools at your disposal. These principles are your anchor in a turbulent sea. The specific technologies will come and go, the market will shift, and the hype will rise and fall. But a business built on a solid foundation of creating genuine value, managed with discipline, and guided by a commitment to learning and adaptation, will not just survive the future. It will be the one that builds it.

* * *

Appendix: Acronyms and Terms for AI Entrepreneurs

This appendix provides brief definitions of commonly used terms and acronyms in this book. It is designed to help new readers build a foundational understanding as they explore the AI startup landscape.

- **AI: Artificial Intelligence** – the simulation of human intelligence in machines.
- **API: Application Programming Interface** – a set of rules that allows different software applications to communicate.
- **B2B: Business to Business** – companies that sell products or services to other businesses.
- **B2B2C: Business to Business to Consumer** – a model combining B2B and B2C transactions.
- **B2C: Business to Consumer** – companies that sell directly to consumers.
- **BI: Business Intelligence** – technologies for analyzing business information.
- **CCPA: California Consumer Privacy Act** – a state-level data privacy law in California.
- **CMS: Content Management System** – software for creating, managing, and modifying digital content.

- **CPRA: California Privacy Rights Act** – an amendment to the CCPA enhancing consumer privacy rights.
- **CRM: Customer Relationship Management** – systems used to manage a company's interactions with current and future customers.
- **CTR: Click-Through Rate** – the percentage of people who click on a link out of the total who view it.
- **EIN: Employer Identification Number** – a unique number assigned to a business entity for tax purposes.
- **FAQ: Frequently Asked Questions** – a list of common questions and answers about a particular topic.
- **GDPR: General Data Protection Regulation** – EU law on data protection and privacy.
- **GTM: Go To Market** – a strategy for launching a product or service to the market.
- **ICP: Ideal Customer Profile** – a detailed description of a company or person most likely to benefit from your product.
- **iPaaS: Integration Platform as a Service** – cloud-based platforms for integrating applications and data.
- **KPI: Key Performance Indicator** – a measurable value that shows how effectively a company is achieving key objectives.
- **LLC: Limited Liability Company** – a business structure that provides limited personal liability to its owners.
- **LLM: Large Language Model** – an AI model trained on vast amounts of text data to understand and generate language.
- **LTV: Lifetime Value** – the total revenue a business expects from a customer over their relationship.
- **Low-Code:** Platforms that require minimal coding to build applications.
- **ML: Machine Learning** – a subset of AI that involves training algorithms on data to make predictions or decisions.
- **MSA: Master Services Agreement** – a contract that outlines terms for future transactions between parties.
- **MVP: Minimum Viable Product** – the simplest version of a product that can be released to test a business idea.

- **NPS: Net Promoter Score** – a metric that gauges customer loyalty and satisfaction.
- **No-Code:** Platforms that allow users to build apps without writing code.
- **ROI: Return on Investment** – a measure used to evaluate the profitability of an investment.
- **SEO: Search Engine Optimization** – improving a website's visibility on search engines.
- **SME: Small and Medium-sized Enterprises** – businesses with limited revenue and number of employees.

or

- **SME: Subject Matter Expert** – individual with a deep knowledge of a subject area such as AI/ML.
- **SOW: Statement of Work** – a document that outlines project-specific activities and deliverables.
- **SaaS: Software as a Service** – cloud-based software accessed via the internet on a subscription basis.
- **TTV: Time To Value** – the time it takes a customer to realize value from a product or service.
- **UI: User Interface** – the visual elements of a product through which a user interacts.
- **URL: Uniform Resource Locator** – the web address of a resource on the internet.
- **UX: User Experience** – how a user interacts with and experiences a product or system.

About the Author

Joseph F. Miceli Jr. has spent more than four decades at the intersection of business strategy and cutting-edge technology. His career spans high-stakes M&A leadership at EMC and IBM, consulting with Microsoft and other global powerhouses, and guiding hundreds of entrepreneurs in transforming raw ideas into thriving enterprises.

A seasoned strategist and technologist, Joseph brings a rare perspective forged from both boardroom negotiations and hands-on innovation. He has seen how disruption reshapes markets, how timing defines success, and how entrepreneurs who act decisively can build lasting companies.

Now, with artificial intelligence unleashing the next trillion-dollar economy, Joseph's converged experience in business growth, enterprise technology, and entrepreneurial execution makes him uniquely equipped to show founders how to seize the moment.

Launch Your A.I. Based Business Today distills his decades of lessons into a practical, battle-tested playbook for anyone ready to turn ambition into action.

You can connect with me on:

🌐 https://jfmicelijr.com

❶ https://www.facebook.com/profile.php?id=61579880879837